North African Cinema in a Global Context

This book provides an insight into contemporary film production from the North African countries referred to as the Maghreb. Focus is on both the socio-economic context of film production, which suffers some of the same setbacks and obstacles as other regions of the developing world, and the thematic details treated in the films themselves. The book delves into ideas such as gender and sexuality, national identity, political conflict, and issues of post and neo-colonial relationships in the context of globalisation.

The book includes close analyses of individual films which show the taboo subjects of sexual and substance abuse, the lives of street children and prostitution, as well as social contradictions of the elite classes who occupy a position of privilege while in the midst of a traditionalist society. Other chapters focus on an individual filmmaker's world view as depicted in representations of contemporary daily life of the average Tunisian, Moroccan or Algerian. The theoretical questions raised include 'third world' art and film production in conditions of political repression and rigid moral conservatism.

This book was previously published as a special issue of *The Journal of North African Studies*.

Andrea Khalil is a professor of Comparative Literature at Queens College, CUNY and of French and Francophone Studies at the Graduate Center, CUNY. She is the author of *The Arab Avant-Garde: Experiments in North African Art and Literature*.

T0314679

North African Cinema in a Global Context

Through the Lens of Diaspora

Edited by Andrea Khalil

Routledge
Taylor & Francis Group

LONDON AND NEW YORK

First published 2008 by Routledge
2 Park Square, Milton Park, Abingdon, Oxfordshire OX14 4RN

Simultaneously published in the USA and Canada
by Routledge
711 Third Avenue, New York, NY 10017

First issued in paperback 2014

Routledge is an imprint of the Taylor & Francis Group, an informa business

Typeset in Times Roman by Techset Composition, Salisbury, UK

British Library Cataloguing in Publication Data
A catalogue record for this book is available from the British Library

ISBN 13: 978-1-138-86464-1 (pbk)
ISBN 13: 978-0-415-46032-3 (hbk)

Contents

Acknowledgements

I would like to express my appreciation for the intelligence and conviviality of all of the contributors of this volume. I have enjoyed working with all of them and hope to continue to work on collective projects in the future. I would also like to thank John Entelis for encouraging me to proceed with this project. Thanks to Ali Ahmed at Queens who has been so supportive of my research and to Dad and Miriam who helped me juggle the kids, writing and teaching this year. Aseel Sawalha's writing support has helped me enormously, making Tuesdays the most productive day of the week. Thanks also to Mohamed, Noha and Ismail for being patient with me when I was absorbed in writing and reading these chapters and for filling my life with joy when I'm not writing.

Andrea Khalil

Introduction

Examining the articles collected in this volume the reader will note that, despite the diverse points of interest, focus and entry into North African cinema, all of the authors are in one way or the other dealing with the relationship between cultural politics internal to North African society and its relation to an 'outside'. This 'outside' is at times France, the old colonial power, and sometimes, increasingly, a more expansive, globalising and hegemonic cultural and political force that both frees and restricts the production of North African cinema. The 'outside' is manifested as both imaginary, in geographical flights as well as flights of fantasy, and very material. Geopolitics, international capital, power, media images flowing in from Hollywood are all 'outside' forms of influence that are increasingly becoming part of the North African filmic imagination.

The dynamics at work in the production and reception of a North African film, these authors demonstrate, at once reach deep into the local culture inhabited and practised by the characters (and filmmakers) but simultaneously move far beyond the very local environments in which they are set. A neighbourhood in Algiers or Casablanca, a family or couple in Sousse: these are the intimate personalities and places which form the scenarios and stages on which the films are shot. But the images, objects, desires and dreams that people the film stretch outside the confines of the sometimes stifling time and place where the characters find themselves. Dreams of 'other' lands, sometimes 'America', the West, or more deterritorialised, imagined places of freedom and phantasm, as in the utopia envisioned in *Ali Zaoua*, circulate in these film narratives.

The current generation of North African filmmakers is no longer directly engaging with 'postcolonial' representations which typically dealt with the tension between the colonies (North Africa) and the coloniser (France). Now, one sees the North African realities that are presented through a more diasporic lens, a geographical and geopolitical splitting suggested in the title of this volume. All of the filmmakers here are part of the Maghrebi diaspora, and travel back and forth between Europe or North America and their North African origins. They look to each shore of the globe's waters with the other shore already imprinted on their field of vision. But the 'other' world is not just the antinomy of 'this' world in a geographical and ethical binary.

Kevin Dwyer focuses on the effective and very practical importance of the 'outside', where international, non-private funding becomes vital for the survival of Moroccan cinema. Third World cinema in general, he explains, exists in a precarious situation given the high-budget, American or other 'First World' productions that circulate easily throughout the world. Globalisation, he continues, puts 'local' cinema at a disadvantage since 'creators in smaller countries experience ever growing difficulty communicating with publics both within and across national borders, as they face competition from internationally produced and distributed works that have immense financial backing'.

He shows the impact of efforts like those of UNESCO's Convention on the Protection and Promotion of the Diversity of Cultural Expressions on Moroccan cinema production.

In Brian Edwards' article, the 'outside' is circulating in recent Moroccan films not through the international policies and sources of funding (although the author does underline the French and European support for production) but rather through the 'look', the American 'style', the 'western' female body type, pop-cultural objects, entertainment and sensibilities that enter into the representation of local Moroccan life through the global movement of culture from the US in the direction of North Africa. The 2005 film *Marock* (directed by Laila Marrakchi) provides Edwards with an opportunity to explain 'the shift in Moroccan representations in the age of global capital and cultural flows'. Edwards' attentiveness to social class, how it is both eclipsed and highlighted in this film about bourgeois Casablancan teenagers, underscores the problem of how economic globalisation produces an international elite while the Moroccan underclass are doubly marginalised first by their forced locality and second by their relation to both an internal and external cultural hegemony.

Robert Lang's analysis of Nouri Bouzid's *Bezness* likewise takes up the subject of how the increasingly global international flow of capital shapes the production of North African cinema, here Tunisian, seeing 'the film as allegorical of Tunisia's precarious economic and cultural position in a rapidly globalising world'. Lang's discussion sheds light on the relationship that surfaces between capitalism's impact on a country such as Tunisia (whose economy is largely sustained by tourism) and the sexual identity and desire of Tunisians. Lang writes, 'Some of the Tunisian cinema's singularity can be found in its willingness—unusual in an Arab society—to present the allegory of the embattled situation of the public Third World culture and society in the private, individual terms of sexuality'. The link that is established in Lang's article between national allegory and individual sexuality opens space for the discussion of the transformation of gender identities thematised in Algerian cinema.

The relationship between geopolitics and sexual identity is the topic continued in both Andrea Khalil's discussion on Merzak Allouache's filmmaking and in Hakim Abderrezak's article on Nadir Moknèche, the former filmmaker working between Algeria and France and the latter working between Algeria, France, Morocco and the United States. Khalil argues that following the social, economic and political disruptions in the postcolonial period ensues a disruption of gender identities, the author focusing specifically on how masculinity has been shaken in the Algerian national narrative. Seeking forms of gender identity and sexuality 'outside' ideological constructions (Islamist, colonialist and orientalist), the characters in Allouache's films seek flight from the suffocating spaces delineated by their gender.

While Khalil looks at the embattled state of Algerian/Arab patriarchy and the effects on masculinity in Algeria, Hakim Abderrezak's study explains how the 'modernisation' of the harem can free traditional female gender roles and allow women to assume positions of social control. Abderrezak carefully defines 'the end of the traditional harem and the initiation of a new social structure ... the modern harem, which manifests itself through a redefinition of masculine and feminine gender roles, a reconfiguration of social space and a recognition of the inevitable effects of modernisation'. The author discusses how female characters use their traditional spaces of confinement as leverage from the margins, becoming subversive agents in a rapidly transforming society where women can empower themselves and dominate men. Abderrezak clarifies that the word 'modern' in Maghrebi Arabic means anything that comes from the West, often also associated with fashionable. Akin to Edwards' notion of circulation, Abderrezak shows the influence of outside, global trends upon the image of the North African woman, or gendered subject generally.

Josef Gugler, in his article on *Ali Zaoua*, locates the experience of the street boys of Casablanca along side other filmic renditions of the global underclass. This film, Gugler notes, simultaneously draws our attention to the situation of a small group of boys in Casablanca, but also to productions such as Luis Bunuel's *Los Olvidas* (Mexico), Hector Babenco's *Pixote* and Fernando Meirelles' *City of God* (Brazil) and Mira Nair's *Salaam Bombay!* (India), thus drawing our eyes both to a very local point of economic and social tension in Morocco but also to a global problem of ever increasing poverty among isolated sectors of the population. The child's visions of a utopia produce an 'other' place of fantasy and dream that make the present realities of poverty and violence liveable.

The way in which politics shapes the production of art and literature is a complex one, entwined in the fabric of the work of art, in the script and direction of a film, embedded in the conscience and production process traversed by a filmmaker. North African film-makers working under such discouraging conditions of material, political and verbal restrictions, all produced by national and geopolitical realities, unable to explicitly express political opinions or sometimes personal desires, enter into a dream-world which, in the most successful of cases, represents a repressed and collective unconscious-ness, and is formalised as a space of the globalising cultural hegemony of the West. Freedom is always imagined, in these films, as 'somewhere else'.

Illustrative of this paradox, the omnipresence of/flight from political repression, is a comment made by Yacef Saadi in *Le Monde*, 13 May 2004. On 19 June 1965, one month after Gillo Pontecorvo had returned to Algiers to start filming *The Battle of Algiers*, Colonel Boumedienne overthrows Ben Bella in a coup, and asks Saadi to serve as a member of his revolutionary council. In response to this request, and, note, about one of the most violently and overtly political films to be made about North Africa, its Algerian writer and producer stated: '*Je ne m'occupe plus de la politique, laissez-moi faire mon film*'. [I no longer deal with politics, let me make my film.]

Andrea Khalil

Moroccan Cinema and the Promotion of Culture

KEVIN DWYER

Introduction

Moroccan and other Third World cinemas operate today in very turbulent conditions, marked not only by changes in their own national environments but also by far-reaching developments on a world scale in technology, economics, politics and culture. There is little consensus about the deeper implications of these developments: some argue that, as communication across the globe becomes easier, we increasingly live in one 'global village'; others counter that creators in smaller countries experience ever growing difficulty communicating with publics both within and across national borders, as they face competition from internationally produced and distributed works that have immense financial backing.

Moroccan cinema constitutes one of the few bright spots in a Third World cinematic landscape that is gloomy at best. However, even in the Moroccan case the signs are ambiguous: while the number of films produced has been increasing, serious problems in film distribution and screening remain. In these circumstances, what is the likelihood that Moroccan filmmakers, and Third World filmmakers in general, will be able to continue to produce films and that these films will reach their own national and perhaps even international audiences? Will it be possible for cultural creation in the Third World to respond to local, national, and regional aspirations or will it be submerged by products from the most powerful metropolitan centres? To explore these questions I will describe how financial support from outside the private sector is a necessary (although not sufficient) condition for the survival of Moroccan and other small national cinemas, and then examine the effort to ensure such non-private support by promoting cultural diversity, in the face of free-trade offensives launched by the world's dominant economic powers.

Moroccan Cinema—Perils and Paradoxes

In Morocco, as in most of the Third World, overall movie attendance is decreasing and theatres are closing or, if remaining open, are showing mostly foreign imports. The relatively small and poor national markets have limited consumer capacity and extremely scarce investment capital, and the national languages in which films are made are viewed as 'local' by international distributors who refuse to market the films abroad. And the many foreign films being shot in Morocco often push aside the nation's own filmmakers, distorting the demand for actors and technicians and encouraging higher fees than local producers can pay. Any one of these factors would make the goal of profit for a Moroccan film recede into the distance; taken together they turn even the more modest aim of recouping investment into a mirage. As a result, Moroccan filmmakers and filmmakers from smaller countries cannot hope to secure more than token private financing and must depend on support from other sources, such as state and/or foreign aid.[1]

Yet even when they find non-private financing and succeed in producing the film, the film sector's basic economics works against their films being shown. International distributors are unwilling to take on such 'local' films, forcing producers to target only their own national distributors, from whom they must seek relatively high payments to offset their costs. But these payments then tend to be higher than those for films from abroad, which have earned money elsewhere and are usually available on the national market at rock-bottom prices. Local distributors thus avoid the national films, knowing that in all likelihood their higher payments for these films will not be offset by higher box-office receipts. In this vicious circle, locally produced films are often not screened and have no chance of recouping costs.

In these circumstances and against all odds, a striking paradox distinguishes the Moroccan situation: under such perilous conditions and with so many fundamental problems affecting filmmaking, a healthy number of Moroccan films has been produced in the past few years and the Moroccan public, which long showed little interest in Moroccan films, has since the 1990s been welcoming these films with great enthusiasm and supporting them at the box-office. In 1999 Moroccan films ranked first, second and ninth in receipts and occupied three of the top five places in admissions. This trend continues— in 2004 the top two films in attendance were Moroccan, as were three of the top four and six of the top ten; in 2006 the top three films in audience and box-office receipts were Moroccan. On the whole, for 2004, the average attendance for a Moroccan film far exceeded attendance for films of all other nationalities, averaging more than three times the number for Indian films and almost five times more than for US films, the national film's two closest competitors. Although Moroccan films made up only 3.7 per cent of films shown in Morocco, they produced 13.5 per cent of box-office revenue (Centre Cinématographique Marocain [CCM] figures).

In the area of film policy there have been a number of positive, although modest, developments in Morocco. In particular, state financial support for films has increased. The main state support to film production comes via the Aid Fund, administered by the

CCM. The amounts awarded have increased significantly in recent years, now reaching a total of 50 million dirhams a year (about $5 million), approximately two and a half times the amount awarded just a few years ago. In addition, the award is now in the form of an 'advance against takings' (resembling the French model) where, rather than treating the sums awarded as non-recoverable, they become an advance to be repaid, at least in part, through a levy on a film's box-office receipts. Amounts recovered in this way are added to the sum available for future awards which, in theory at least, provides some guarantee that support will continue. However, it is not yet clear whether the proposed funding increases will be sustained over an extended period nor whether these modifications in the Aid Fund, without corresponding reforms in distribution and exhibition, will have a positive effect overall. In the best of cases Moroccan cinema would be in a good position to approach the official middle term target of 15–20 features per year. constituting a significant advance on past achievement. However, distribution and exhibition—keys to the health of the film sector—continue to constitute weak points, with Moroccan distributors and exhibitors persisting in preferring foreign imports and resisting policies that support national films.

Other recent policy developments include the announcement, in 2005, that the two existing Moroccan television stations would each increase their commitment to films so that a total of some 30 films per year—television films and feature films—would be produced or co-produced with the stations' financial aid, thus enabling television to become a main workplace for film professionals and add to the corpus of Moroccan films. There has also been a strengthening of the legal status of artists, improvements in copyright law (Fr. *les droits d'auteur*), and increased vigilance against piracy.[2] Two new film schools were planned (in Ouarzazate and Marrakesh) whereas, until recently, there had been none at all; and a series of collaborative seminars, workshops and conferences were set up in conjunction with the European Union under its EuroMed programme and the Tribeca Film Festival, enabling aspiring Moroccan film students to enter into contact with and to benefit from the experiences of world-class filmmakers like Martin Scorsese and Abbas Kiarostami. Morocco also introduced, in 2001, its own annual international film festival, held in Marrakesh and reaching its sixth session at the end of 2006. Attracting celebrities from all over, this festival has enabled Morocco to gain greater visibility in the international film world, adding to the visibility already achieved as a result of the country's role as a location for foreign films, and providing a heightening of film consciousness that complements the cinephilia stimulated by Morocco's own national film festivals.[3]

Most importantly for the future of Moroccan cinema, works by the younger generation of filmmakers have been received very positively—these include Faouzi Ben Saidi (b. 1967), Hakim Belabbes (b. 1961), Narjess Nejjar (b. 1971), Laila Marrakchi (b. 1975), Noureddin Lekhmari (b. 1964), Ismail Ferroukhi (b. 1962), Yasmine Kassari (b. 1968), Nabyl Ayouch (b. 1969), among others. Many of these filmmakers have roots in one (or more) societies in addition to Morocco; also, there has been a significant increase, among this younger generation, in the number of women filmmakers, whereas, with the notable exception of Farida Benlyazid (b.1948), women were largely absent from the older generation.

All these developments are taking place in a political and social situation that is relatively encouraging. While the public freedoms to discuss, criticise and mobilise in defence of objectives that might challenge authority are sometimes curtailed, and while most Moroccans are consciously and subconsciously aware of the 'red lines' that are dangerous to cross, the freedom that Moroccans have come to enjoy in the public sphere, and in Moroccan cinema as one of its most important sectors, has expanded significantly in recent years when compared to previous decades. This greater freedom in the field of cinema can be seen, for example, in the strength of the theme of political repression and political criticism that has been strongly in evidence in a number of recent Moroccan films. Censorship, although always a possibility, has been imposed infrequently. In one notable recent incident a film by Nabyl Ayouch, *A Minute of Sun Less* (2003), was ruled unsuitable for screening unless several scenes were shortened or cut. The filmmaker refused and the film was not allowed in the theatres. On the other hand, Laila Marrakchi's very controversial film *Marock* (2005) was released uncensored although restricted to viewers over 12 years of age, and became the highest grossing film in Morocco in 2006.

Promoting Cultural Diversity

All in all, with ample talent on hand, a younger generation keen to take up the mantle, and the government projecting increased financial support for film production, much would seem to be in place for continued growth and an increasingly dynamic Moroccan film sector. Yet there are also serious obstacles: infrastructural, financial, the size of the market, social problems of poverty, illiteracy and unemployment, to name a few. There is also a rather hostile global environment that makes the cinemas of small producers like Morocco exceedingly vulnerable. All things considered, although there are many promising signs, there are no conclusive reasons for believing that they foreshadow a rosy future.

This raises a more general ethical and philosophical question, for which Morocco provides a particularly interesting example: what is the outlook for promoting diversity of cultural expression and production in a world media landscape dominated by large-scale producers, where creators in smaller countries have to struggle against great odds to reach their publics and where it is extremely difficult to establish the institutions and policies necessary to encourage creative activity?

In the international arena there is much controversy over this issue, which was first phrased with reference to the notion of '*cultural exception*' (the view that cultural products should be excluded from international free-trade agreements and that states should be permitted to subsidise cultural production and adopt related supportive measures) and more recently invoked the concept of 'cultural diversity' (that cultural diversity is of primordial significance to all of humanity and requires active promotion and protection). Whereas the 'cultural exception' betrays a defensive posture, 'cultural diversity' implies a more 'offensive' stance, suggesting a broad constructive effort to provide an ethical and legal foundation for the promotion of cultural expression and production. This fundamental ethico-philosophical question thus revolves around whether cultural products should be treated as simple commercial commodities and thus subject to free-trade provisions, or whether they deserve special encouragement and protection.

Audiovisual productions, feature films among them, have been a main focus of this discussion for a number of reasons:

1. audiovisual productions in general, and feature films in particular, are extremely vulnerable to free-trade provisions since they require massive investment at the point

of creation (in contrast to poetic and literary productions, for example), and removing financial aid mechanisms would cripple production;

2. audiovisual productions are easy to package and market, both locally and internationally, and are capable of generating significant profits;

3. audiovisual products appear to some interest groups to be similar to other 'entertainment' activities and therefore to be simply one commodity among others, objects for consumption—this view denies such products the specific cultural value usually attached to products of 'high culture'.

Much of the controversy over this question and much of the effort to establish an ethical and legal foundation for cultural diversity—for the right to give special treatment to cultural expression and production—has taken place within the framework of the United Nations Educational, Scientific, and Cultural Organisation (UNESCO). In late 2001 UNESCO adopted unanimously a *Universal Declaration on Cultural Diversity*, which argues that 'cultural diversity is as necessary for humankind as biodiversity is for nature' (Article 1) and proposes to safeguard this diversity both in relations between societies and in activity within them, thus tying cultural diversity to the fundamental human rights of creative freedom and freedom of expression. More specifically, UNESCO's declaration states that 'cultural goods and services [are] commodities of a unique kind ... which, as vectors of identity, values and meaning, must not be treated as mere commodities or consumer goods' (Article 8).

Within UNESCO, a large group of countries, led by France and Canada, moved to transform this declaration into an international convention that would provide enforceable legal provisions (as is the case with other international conventions, such as the International Convention on Civil and Political Rights) and would enable legal constraints to be imposed on organisations such as the WTO. The US was absent from UNESCO in 2001 when these initiatives first took shape but rejoined in late 2003, after an absence of some 20 years.[4] With the US having consistently promoted the view that cultural goods and services are commodities like any other, the effort to elaborate an international convention on cultural diversity was unlikely to go smoothly.

In October 2005, the battle was joined when, at the 33rd General Conference of UNESCO, a Convention on the Protection and Promotion of the Diversity of Cultural Expressions was put to a vote. In the weeks just preceding the vote, the US delegation proposed a significant number of amendments and US Secretary of State Condoleezza Rice addressed a letter to all foreign ministers members of UNESCO, requesting that they prolong discussion and postpone voting, expressing her concern that 'ambiguous formulations' would block all progress toward the liberalisation of trade.[5]

In the event, the Convention was adopted by an overwhelming vote—151 states for, four abstentions (Australia, Honduras, Nicaragua and Liberia), and two against (the US and Israel). Even Japan, which had earlier in the process indicated its opposition, voted in favour; and the UK, a strong ally of the US on many trade-related issues, supported the Convention, with its ambassador to UNESCO, speaking for the EU, saying that the draft was 'clear, carefully balanced, and consistent with the principles of international law and fundamental human rights'.[6]

Some of the major principles embodied in this Convention include 'respect for human rights and fundamental freedoms' (Article 2); promoting 'openness to other cultures' (Article 2); encouraging internal minority expression (Article 8); offering preferential treatment for developing countries (Article 16); establishing an international fund to promote cultural diversity (Article 18); positing a complementary, non-subordinate relationship with other international agreements (Article 20); and setting up a (non-binding) dispute settlement procedure (Article 25).[7]

Conditions are now ripe for a number of further battles, and some of them are already looming. Among these one can foresee wrangling over the question of ratification, the likelihood of cases for dispute settlement within the Convention, and disagreements that will no doubt arise over how to interpret the Convention's relations with other treaties, in particular with the WTO. Let me deal briefly with each of these.

According to Article 29, the Convention enters into effect after it has been ratified by 30 member states. There was little doubt that countries opposed to the Convention, particularly the US, would use their influence to discourage ratification.[8] Nonetheless, by 18 December 2006 the requisite number of states had ratified and the Convention entered into force on 18 March 2007.

Even with the Convention's entry into force, there may be disputes between states within the framework of the Convention itself, as a consequence of tensions between various articles, such as those that recognise the sovereign rights of states and those requiring states to respect human rights instruments and the principle of openness and balance. Disagreements here would lead to application of the dispute settlement procedure.

Finally, with respect to other treaty obligations and particularly those under the WTO, the likelihood of conflict is very high. Already there are major differences of interpretation in the meaning of Article 20 on non-subordination and complementarity. The British, who approved the Convention, argue that this article in no way allows cultural goods to be withdrawn from the domain of the WTO; for the French and for a number of NGOs, this article provides a clear basis for such withdrawals.[9]

And then there are a number of criticisms that may be made of the Convention itself. These come from both camps—from those who, like the US representatives, believe that the Convention oversteps its area of responsibility and from those who argue that the Convention does not go far enough. From the first camp, we hear the basic argument that all matters dealing with trade in goods and services are within the purview of the WTO and that, therefore, the Convention has no standing to interfere in these matters. The principle usually advanced to support this position is that freedom of expression is paramount and that all people should be allowed to exercise free choice in the forms of expression they wish to consume.[10] In the particular context of the audiovisual this praiseworthy principle strongly favours powerful economic actors, given the clear relationship that exists between economic power and the capacity to promote (i.e. market) expression in the public sphere. And the US would be its prime beneficiary, since 'The US currently enjoys overwhelming superiority in the international trade of cultural goods and services, most of the world's media conglomerates responsible for film and television production [are] ... based in the US ... [and bring in] nearly 2/3 of the ... revenues generated by the media industry worldwide'.[11] Other criticisms from this camp attack, as Condoleezza Rice did, the 'vague' nature of the terms used in the Convention. For example, Dan Glickman, president of the Motion Picture Association of America (the main lobbying group for Hollywood interests), expressed concern that 'any country negotiating trade agreements might argue that there are cultural perspectives embodied in coffee, bananas, cotton, or cheese'.[12]

From those who believe the Convention is too weak come criticisms that, in the final text, (1) the Fund for Cultural Diversity is only voluntary; (2) the early drafts had stronger obligations, with phrases like 'States must', whereas the final text reads 'States should'[13]; and (3) this conditional wording will make it difficult to put into effect the Convention's Article 20 on non-subordination because the obligations under WTO are much more constraining.[14] Finally, there is the deeper question of whether the emphasis in Article 20 on non-subordination and complementarity should be the way forward or, on the other hand, should the protection and promotion of cultural expression directly challenge the notions of free trade embodied in World Trade Organisation treaties.[15]

In sum, the criticisms from the various quarters see the Convention as seriously flawed—vague in many places, open to conflict, insufficiently constraining, inadequately financed, and without any binding dispute settlement procedure.

In this context, what is the outlook for a Third World cinema like Morocco's? If the Convention on the Protection and Promotion of the Diversity of Cultural Expressions remains weak or even a dead letter and WTO principles strengthen, a state's capacity to protect and promote its own film production would be severely crippled. There are two principles in free-trade policies that are especially relevant here. The first is that all foreign-made products should be treated equally to domestic ones. This would make it impossible for governments to provide aid and facilities to national films, since such support would have to be made available to any foreign film—in Morocco's case national films would be competing with such recent big-budget foreign films made in Morocco as Ridley Scott's *Black Hawk Down* and *Gladiator*, and, most recently, Alejandro González Iñárittu's *Babel*.

The second principle is the 'most favoured nation' principle—that any favourable treatment accorded by one nation to another should be extended to all nations. This would rule out supportive measures included in bilateral trade agreements (for example, the aid France provides to Third World—and Moroccan—cinemas would have to be discontinued, since it could not possibly be extended to all countries). Clearly, to subject cultural productions such as film to these kinds of free-trade regimes would undermine the support the film sector needs from its society's institutions and would undermine, even more fundamentally, the capacity of societies to set their own priorities. Such a regime also transparently skews the system in favour of the large-scale producers and their advantages in marketing, distribution, etc. Bearing in mind the precarious situation of almost all small national cinemas, one can easily imagine the destructive effects of applying these principles and/or proposals such as the one formulated by the World Trade Organisation that state support for film production be limited to 5 per cent of costs.[16]

However, the WTO is itself subject to increasingly serious strains that limit its power to promote free trade to the exclusion of other values. In 2001, as increasing membership of Third World countries led to their growing influence, the so-called Doha Round was initiated, in which developing countries' concerns were to receive the highest priority. Disagreements over measures supported by many Third World countries, such as liberalisation of trade in agricultural products, were opposed in varying degrees by the US, western Europe, and Japan, leading to the organisation's partial paralysis. In response, several of the major powers, and the US in particular, have sought bilateral accords where it is easier for them to obtain the free-trade provisions they prefer. Among the countries with which the US has already negotiated or is in the process of negotiating bilateral free-trade agreements that limit aid provided to the audiovisual sector are Honduras, Nicaragua, Colombia, Ecuador, Peru, Thailand and, last but not least, Morocco.[17]

Conclusion

There are, in the global film world, some successful experiences by small national cinemas such as Brazil, South Korea and Nigeria, where, for a variety of reasons including an encouraging legal environment, the institution of quotas in the theatres, and allowing the development of video distribution circuits, significant advances have been made. Many of the measures adopted in these countries and in countries such as France that strongly promote their film sectors could be adopted by Morocco and other Third World countries. Financing, legal structures, and institutional arrangements to encourage national production and exhibition might also be instituted to encourage regional co-ordination (and, eventually, 'South–South' co-operation), which would aid the survival of national cinemas. In fact, both the CCM and Moroccan television stations have recently been involved in co-producing several Algerian and Tunisian films.

While many supportive measures can be envisaged, these often involve trade-offs and one needs to ask where Moroccan cinema will fit in the priorities of the Moroccan government, the Palace, and Moroccans themselves, given the seriousness of the country's social problems. What kinds of policies toward the film sector and cultural production in general will be elaborated and implemented? Even were substantial financial support for film production to continue, will that support be supplemented by measures in the areas of distribution and screening, and will all this contribute to reinforcing the now well-consolidated 'reconciliation' between Moroccan audiences and Moroccan films?

There are many reasons to maintain the hope that Moroccan cinema will retain the energy, creativity, and diversity that have been such important factors in its growth, its recent success, and its promise. The work of some of Morocco's senior filmmakers, and the production among the younger generation of challenging short films and features, many of them displaying stylistic, formal, and thematic originality, simultaneously enhance Morocco's artistic achievements, challenge and enrich Moroccan society and culture, and attract Moroccan audiences—all signs that the sector has great flexibility and the potential to produce significant and affecting works.

Whether Moroccan cinema will see a strengthening of its independence, creativity, and audience relationship will certainly depend on filmmakers' own actions and those of other actors in the Moroccan film world—not least on the attitudes of those responsible for financing, distribution, and screening and for creating an encouraging legal and administrative context. But it will also depend on social, cultural and political developments beyond the film sector, such as whether educational levels will rise, freedom of expression will expand, disposable income will increase, all of which would contribute to growth in the internal market.

However, while such actions and developments are necessary, they may not be sufficient, for it is an unanswered question whether the strengthening of cinema is possible in a country situated as Morocco is with regard to the global marketplace, even if internal factors work in positive directions. But at least we can suggest that currently, with Moroccan cinema benefiting from the groundwork and structures built by its pioneers, with Moroccan films' box-office success continuing, with a new generation of talented Moroccan and diasporic filmmakers, and with a political and cultural system rapidly changing in mostly encouraging directions, Morocco is very well positioned to provide an instructive lesson concerning whether this particular national cinema, and Third World cinemas more generally, can grow in their domestic markets and reach international audiences as well.

Notes

1. There were only 141 theatres in Morocco at the start of 2005 (counting multiplex cinemas according to their number of screens), down by more than 40 per cent from a high of 247 in 1985. Attendance has also dropped precipitously, from 45 million admissions in 1980 to under 11 million in 2002 and less than five million in 2005. More recent figures show these trends continuing, even accelerating: provisional figures from the Centre Cinématographique Marocain (CCM) show the number of theatres decreasing to 115 in 2006 and to under 80 by early 2007, and attendance figures continue to drop. These reductions appear even more extreme when seen relative to population, which has increased over the past 25 years by more than 50 per cent. Foreign features filmed in Morocco during 2002—to take a recent, rather typical year—invested 12 times more than Moroccan features, employed eight times as many technicians, almost twice as many actors, and 30 times as many extras. If all genres are included (features and short films, advertising spots, video clips, etc.), foreign productions accounted for approximately 90 per cent of investment in 2002 (all figures here are from the CCM).
2. With DVD/video sales constituting a significant portion of a film's income (in the US, for example, income from video/DVD made up almost 60 per cent of the domestic film revenue in the US for the year 2002 (Taub, 2003), the battle against piracy is an important one. Recent experience shows that it has been possible to go to almost any major marketplace in urban Morocco and buy DVDs of major international films for 15–20 DH ($1.50–2.00), but that may now be changing as a result of the anti-piracy offensive.
3. The Marrakesh International Film Festival also often offers, in a separate section, a panorama of Moroccan films, enabling the international audience at the festival to gain some knowledge of the national cinema. Since 1982 Morocco has had its own National Film Festival and it has been held at irregular intervals ever since, each time showing all (or almost all) national films produced in the intervening period. Two clear trends appear since the 1982 event: first, the festivals are now being held at more regular and frequent intervals (every two to three years) and second, the rate of film production has been increasing. At the three most recent festivals one could see, in Marrakesh in 2001, 15 features and 17 shorts; in Oujda in 2003, 16 features and 17 shorts; and in Tangiers in 2005, some 20 features and 40 shorts. The next National Film Festival is scheduled for 2007. Among other film festivals in Morocco we find the Festival of Maghreb Films held in Oujda, the Festival of African Films (Khouribga), the Festival of Mediterranean Cinema (Tetouan), the Festival of Short Films (Tangiers), the Festival of Women's Films (Salé) and the International Festival of Animated Films (Meknes).
4. It had left in 1984, along with the UK, following disagreement over several UNESCO programmes, including UNESCO's support for the 'New World Information and Communication Order' that the US criticised as anti-western and supportive of censorship and state control over media.
5. Rice stated that 'We believe that this convention could also be used by certain governments to restrict the free circulation of information and prohibit minority points of view and cultural practices' (*Le Devoir*, 2005).
6. Henley (2005), quoting the ambassador.
7. In a little more detail: Article 2, 'Guiding Principles', states the principle that 'Cultural diversity can be protected and promoted only if human rights and fundamental freedoms ... are guaranteed. No one may invoke the provisions of this Convention in order to infringe human rights ...'; this article also gives the Convention an international perspective in the 'Principle of openness and balance', which states that States 'should seek to promote ... openness to other cultures of the world ...' Article 8, dealing with the internal aspect of minority or threatened cultural expressions, stipulates that states 'may take appropriate measures to protect and preserve cultural expressions ... that are at risk of extinction, under serious threat, or ... in need of urgent safeguarding'. Article 16, in proposing that 'Preferential treatment [be given] for developing countries', says that 'developed countries shall facilitate cultural exchanges with developing countries by granting ... preferential treatment to artists and other cultural professionals ... as well as cultural goods and services from developing countries'. Article 20, dealing with the relationship between this Convention and other international agreements, such as those of the WTO, states the principle of non-subordination to other instruments and the aim of complementarity and mutual supportiveness. There is also the somewhat ominous provision, that 'nothing in this Convention shall be interpreted as modifying rights and obligations of the Parties under any other treaties to which they are parties'.
8. One US State Department official indicated, in late 2005, that the United States could 'try to prevent' states from ratifying the Convention, or 'make sure states do not abuse it' (cited in <http://

www.mcc.gouv.qc.ca/diversite-culturelle/eng/declarations/dc05-10-24.htm>). Another indicated that the United States would resort to bilateral agreements if its initiatives to create free-trade regions were to fail, stating 'if we cannot achieve free trade multilaterally, we'll do it bilaterally' (US ambassador to Argentina, speaking about the Free Trade Area of the Americas, cited in <http://www.mcc.gouv.qc.ca/diversite-culturelle/eng/declarations/dc05-10-24.htm>).

9. 'Pour les Britanniques, l'article 20 ne signifie aucunement que la convention permette de retirer les biens culturels du champ de l [OMC]. Les promoteurs français du texte et les organisations non gouvernementales qui se sont mobilisées ... pour la diversité culturelle ... soutiennent exactement le contraire' (Nougayrède, 2005).
10. As, for example, in the statement of Louise Oliver, US ambassador to UNESCO, that the Convention could be used '"to control—not facilitate—the flow of goods, services and ideas ... [states could use the convention] to control the cultural lives of their citizens ... to control what citizens can see, what they can read, what they can listen to and what they can do" by interfering with the free market and "the right of all people to make these decisions for themselves"'(Tresilian, 2005).
11. Tresilian (2005).
12. 'La convention sur la diversité culturelle inquiète Hollywood' (2005).
13. Michel (2005).
14. Vulser (2005).
15. For this argument, see Michel (2005).
16. The question of whether systematic application of free-trade principles would promote 'development' in poorer countries is too complicated for us to examine here. However, I share the central argument of many writers on the subject who argue that free trade, in itself, is not necessarily conducive to development but may be made so only if designed and implemented in ways that make the needs of poorer countries central.
17. Michel (2005).

References

Henley, J. (2005) Global Plan to Protect Film Culture, *The Guardian*, 19 October.
La convention sur la diversité culturelle inquiète Hollywood (2005) *Le Monde*, 23 October, <http://www.mcc.gouv.qc.ca/diversite-culturelle/eng/declarations/dc05-10-24.htm>.
Le Devoir (2005) 25 October, <http://www.mcc.gouv.qc.ca/diversite-culturelle/eng/international/in05-10-11.htm>.
Michel, C. (2005) Armer la culture face au commerce, *Le Monde*, 19 October.
Nougayrède, N. (2005) La bataille diplomatique et les efforts d'obstruction des E-U ont paradoxalement amplifié la résonance de la convention, *Le Monde*, 19 October.
Taub, E. (2003) Movie DVDs that are Meant for Buying but Not for Keeping, *New York Times*, 21 July.
Tresilian, D. (2005) Solitary at UNESCO, *Ahram Weekly*, 27 October.
Vulser, N. (2005) L'UNESCO adopte le texte sur la diversité culturelle, *Le Monde*, 19 October.

Marock in Morocco: Reading Moroccan Films in the Age of Circulation

BRIAN T. EDWARDS

Rocking the Casa

'The film of all taboos', it was called by its sympathisers. In the late spring of 2006, a controversial new film named *Marock* was all over the Moroccan papers and culture magazines. Made by a 29-year-old Moroccan woman named Laila Marrakchi, who had left Casablanca for France a decade earlier, the film was released in Morocco on 10 May 2006, a year after it had premiered at the Cannes film festival, and a month after its general release in France. These dynamics—a director with a Moroccan upbringing but a French address, and a film about Morocco with French funding and a European provenance—would haunt the film. In Morocco, its arrival on local screens was heralded with the sort of media coverage of an American *succès de scandale*, with the free publicity from excessive news coverage obviating the need for paid advertising. Indeed there were multiple parallels to Hollywood films, both within the film itself with its Hollywood look and American teen movie soundtrack, and in its wide distribution via both formal and informal circuits. Soon after its run at cinemas in Casablanca, Rabat, Fez and Marrakech, contraband copies of the film were available for sale on the sidewalks of Moroccan cities, where it stood alongside pirated copies of Hollywood blockbusters such as *Syriana*, *Jarhead*, Spielberg's *Munich*, *Ice Age 2* and *Cars*, to name those with the broadest informal circulation in June–July 2006.[1] But if part of the surprise about *Marock*'s reception in Morocco was just how Hollywood it all seemed, the controversies it provoked in Morocco revolved around the representations of Moroccan particularity within it. That was the problem.

Marock, Marrakchi's first feature, built on a theme she had explored in her first film, a 12-minute short called *L'Horizon perdu* (2000) about a young man broken by life in the Tangier medina who leaves Morocco for Spain in clandestine fashion. In the case of *Marock*, however, the protagonist's departure from the homeland is deferred for a full 90 minutes and comes at the conclusion of a coming-of-age tale. Though the protagonist is no less broken by her milieu than in the short, in *Marock* the character's elite socio-economic status is never in jeopardy and the emigration is legal and transparent (the last spoken word of the film is the passport control officer's demand, 'Passport', which causes no anxiety). Nearly everything that precedes this final word justifies the departure, which comes both as a relief and as the tearful leave taking from adolescence and Morocco alike. The 17-year-old female protagonist's departure from Morocco was not, however, what made *Marock* controversial, even though the film associates Morocco itself with adolescence and departure from Morocco with the process of maturing. (To be sure, the fact that the director herself had emigrated to France was repeated by the film's detractors.[2]) Rather, what was provocative was the director's frank portrayal of premarital sexuality among elite Casablancans and her flaunting of religious and cultural conventions.

Three plot strands in particular stood out: the open refusal of the protagonist Rita (played by Morjana Alaoui) to fast during the month of Ramadan, when the film is set; Rita's mockery of her brother Mao (Assad El Bouab) at prayer; and her open affair with a Jewish teenager, Youri (Matthieu Boujenah), an affair that is apparently consummated sexually. As the last plot element suggests, the frank treatment of teenage Moroccan sexuality and a disregard for the sanctities of religious tradition were, in *Marock*, deeply intertwined. Across the board, the moment in the film that most disturbed commentators was an intimate scene between Youri and Rita, the two entangled in each other's arms kissing in an isolated seaside shed. Youri, following Rita's eyes to the silver Star of David he wears around his neck, removes the chain and places it around the Muslim girl's neck. 'This way', he says, 'you won't have to think about it'. The film's defenders, such as the liberal cultural magazines *Tel Quel* and *Le Journal Hebdomadaire*, both of which put it on the magazine's cover and dedicated long articles to it, found this the most difficult aspect to watch. Those individuals who supported the film, and those who continue to champion it, still find it difficult to reconcile that disregard for religious decorum.[3] Its detractors used the moment as evidence that the film was part of a Zionist plot and were quick to discredit her. Strong criticism was delivered to Marrakchi in person in Tangier, where the film was screened at the national film festival in December 2005, and in cyberspace, where an active discussion about the film took place among the Moroccan diaspora in France on the French release of the film in February 2006, wherein Marrakchi was taken to task for claiming to speak on behalf of the young generation of Moroccans.[4]

In the public debate that ensued upon the film's general release in Morocco, *Marock* and Marrakchi herself quickly came to stand for multiple positions—freedom of speech, the young 'rock' generation, intellectual and artistic honesty, and humanism, on the one hand, and disrespect for Moroccan tradition, diasporic elitism cut off from the homeland, neo-colonialist pandering to Europe's Islamophobic preoccupations, and savvy self-publicity/provocation, on the other. We might note that these positions are not mutually exclusive. The debate itself, of course, is the first thing to understand. The anxieties that *Marock* provoked were intense across the cultural and political spectrum. The ways in which it was received—the misapprehensions about its novelty or its crimes against the nation—offer a lens through which to make sense of Moroccan culture in the middle of the first decade of the twenty-first century. Whatever the validity of the critiques of the film's aesthetic quality (see Dahan, 2006), therefore, or whatever the anachronism of its attempt to offer a national allegory of twenty-first century Morocco via a tale of departure (which recalled mid-twentieth century modes of the late colonial and early postcolonial period), we should not ignore the film. This is, to be sure, not the same as the American marketing adage that any publicity is good publicity. *Marock* struck a nerve. And if Marrakchi herself predicted that it would do so in a statement made in France before the film had made it to Moroccan screens, a comment which of course antagonised in itself, her success in so doing is no less important to understand.

The Age of Circulation

Marock deserves our attention not only for the debates it occasioned, but also because it is a film text that makes vivid a variety of intertwined features of urban Morocco in the era of globalisation. By 'globalisation', an overused and frequently undertheorised term that is especially subject to what Edward Said called 'travelling theory', I mean something akin to the use of the term by cultural anthropologists who are sensitive both to economic and demographic change and to the category of the imagination. Namely, globalisation is the accelerated transnational movement of capital that follows the world wide shift away from nationally anchored currencies in 1973. 'Globalisation' is also the episteme that emerges during this period—the cultural imaginaries that are formed by subjects brought into new communication by a variety of digital technologies and accelerated or enhanced transport of bodies, images, finances and ideas (Appadurai, 1996, 2001). Benjamin Lee and Edward LiPuma have announced this cultural shift in even starker terms: 'The advent of circulation-based capitalism, along with the social forms and technologies that complement it, signifies more than a shift in emphasis. It constitutes a new stage in the history of capitalism' (2002, p. 210). If we are to take this proposition seriously, which I think we must, there will need to be a reassessment of social forms—including art, literature, cinema, etc.—that emerge within this new stage. Needless to say, this would be a major undertaking.

In their groundbreaking essay, Lee and LiPuma provide an analysis of the forms of collective agency that emerge from within different economic stages in the history of capitalism. Their attempt is to show how the transition from gift-exchange societies (pre-market capitalism) to market capitalism to 'globalisation' after the demise of the gold standard and the floating of currencies creates different forms of imagining the relationship of the individual to the collective and, therefore, different forms of social organisation (see also LiPuma and Lee, 2004). Theirs is a technical analysis that brings together structuralist and poststructuralist linguistic theories of performativity and economic analysis of financial derivatives—the latter are understood as akin to performative speech acts in that they call into being the world they name and thus shape the (economic) future. At stake for critics of contemporary cinema is Lee and LiPuma's claim that analyses of contemporary 'culture', particularly those that attend to 'meaning and interpretation as the key problems for social and cultural analysis', are playing 'catch-up to the economic processes that go beyond it' (2002, p. 191). This statement poses a direct challenge to those who would analyse cultural production since the transition to globalisation, whatever the location where the cultural object is produced.

Lee and LiPuma's essay has resonated through work in transnational cultural studies, though its implications on literary and film studies have not yet been adequately considered. This may be because their challenge to prevailing modes of reading film and literary texts of the past three decades is direct, on the one hand, and not spelled out, on the other. Following Lee and LiPuma's essay, Dilip Gaonkar and Elizabeth Povinelli (2003, p. 388) have addressed the implications of attending to circulation for the analysis of public cultural texts, events and practices and called for attention to the 'dynamic transfiguration of forms across circulatory matrices'. They go yet further with respect to the velvet trap of interpretation when they suggest that critics resist the 'tempta-tion of reading for meaning' and instead pay greater attention to 'the proliferating copre-sence of varied textual/cultural forms in all their mobility and mutability' (pp. 386, 391).

In this essay, it should by now be clear, I would like to take up the challenge of recon-sidering Moroccan cinema from a perspective that attends to its relationship to 'cultures of circulation'. What this will mean with respect to a film such as *Marock* or indeed contem-porary Moroccan cinema in general is straightforward enough. First, that we should attend to the ways in which such films operate within diverse Moroccan media worlds pervaded by the global flow of images, visual technologies and representations. And second, that we must consider the ways in which such films address, create and sometimes mystify Moroccan publics who are confronted on a daily basis with the struggles and conditions posed by the Moroccan encounter with economic globalisation.

Following Lee and LiPuma's lead, then, an expanded sense of 'globalisation' will allow us to specify what is particular about the past three decades and to establish a framework within which to analyse literature, film and other forms of cultural production that are created within such a changed environment. Globalisation conceived of merely as trans-national trade and the cross-border contact of bodies and ideas may be as old as trade or the world system itself (Frank, 1998; see also Arrighi, 1994), but since the mid-1970s, the combination of financial deregulation and technological innovation has sped up these processes at exponential, asymptotic rates. That combination has exacerbated the number of dislocated peoples even while it has allowed for new experiences of the age-old conditions of dislocation and diaspora. In other words, the same people who are put in accelerated motion in pursuit of financial possibilities or in flight from political and economic crises have the possibilities to remain in a particular form of contact because of digital technologies that have been so quickly developed in this period. This leads to specific forms of diasporic experience and new forms of cross-diasporic commu-nity, as Hamid Naficy (1993) has shown in his important work on diasporic media and the cross-ethnic diasporic communities they form in Los Angeles in the 1980s and early 1990s. Such work can be extended to the digital environment of the later 1990s and 2000s, wherein Internet chatrooms, web sites and blogs bring together not only diverse diasporic communities, but put into contact (sometimes uneasy contact) members of the diaspora and nation itself. Said Graiouid's (2005) thinking about what he calls 'virtual *h'rig*' in the Moroccan cybersphere has explored what sorts of immobilities can also come along with the perceived mobility of the Internet.

Shana Cohen and Larabi Jaidi's recent consideration (2006) of the Moroccan encounter with globalisation is particularly useful in attending to the interplay of economic and political pressures from outside and the protean forms that the Moroccan kingdom has assumed in responding to the pulls and pressures of development. One of their findings that will prove particularly useful for my purposes in this essay is the ways in which Moroccan youth have, despite an environment that seems most closely poised toward political inclusion, retrenched into a cultural apathy and apoliticism. For Cohen and Jaidi, Moroccan youth may be seen in the terms of what Susan Ossman (2002) has called 'lightness' of bodies, in her own important study of the transnational circulation of forms of beauty between Casablanca, Paris and Cairo. And though they are focused on economic and political processes, Cohen and Jaidi suggest some of the forms of cultural production that may be implicated by attention to Morocco's complex relationship to globalisation when they focus their attention briefly on a diasporic, anonymous Moroccan rapper who challenges from afar the cultural contradictions of Moroccan national culture.

If what we mean by 'globalisation' implicates an impossibly broad fabric, it is necessary to localise our attentions on particular texts and contexts in order to understand how such a changed or changing episteme works on the imaginary. This critical tactic need not reject Gaonkar and Povinelli's (2003) warning about the dangerous captivation that 'meaning' can pose. Indeed, by attending to the global flow of a Hollywood 'look' or 'form', and the ways in which a filmmaker's work both attends to and is caught up in the circulation of commodities and diasporic-national ideas, we may make progress toward better understanding how 'cultures of circulation' work within the Moroccan context of the past decade. Work such as Naficy's on TV (1993) and Graiouid's on cyberculture (2005) shows how this might be done and what is to be gained by so doing. And despite the ways in which television and cyberculture highlight the technological changes in the environment within which subjectivities operate in the late twentieth and early twenty-first centuries, we need not only attend to new media in order to see such a shift. We may see a marked shift in cultural production more generally. Furthermore, such concerns are made visible within cultural production, sometimes in the media within which they are produced—as with the digital pirate-artist Miloudi, whose montage VCDs from 2003 to 2005, half-CGI Hollywood clips, half-Moroccan *chaabi* music, seemed to create a new art form (see Schultheis, 2005), and also blogs and chatrooms—and sometimes thematically in works created in more traditional media. When 'older' media are chosen by artists as means of expression, we may see a cultural shift in a variety of ways, both thematically and stylistically, as well as the changed environment within which such traditional media now operate. For these reasons, it may be especially useful to examine such 'older' media (cinema, novels, etc.) to understand better the shifts surrounding the choice of media itself.[5]

In any case, if we are to continue reading critically and analysing cinema produced after the shift I am describing, we must avoid doing so armed only with the critical modes developed within the prior episteme. This will mean attention to a variety of factors, both internal and external to the film texts themselves. When so doing, for example, we must not neglect to note the new technologies within which those older forms circulate, are marketed, or are discussed. Thus for *Marock*, the importance of the discussion of the film in Internet chatrooms, and of its distribution first by digital pirates, and eventually by YouTube, and for fiction, its marketing via Amazon, authors' blogs and web sites, to say nothing of the fact that many read such fiction (or snippets of it) via the free pages available on <Amazon.com>. But as we'll see, such concerns also figure largely within many recent Moroccan works in these 'older' media. Watching a feature film such as *Marock* on YouTube, or on digitally pirated copies purchased off the street, or on a laptop computer in a train, on a plane, or lying in bed, one wonders whether it is correct to consider the 'feature film' an 'older' form of cultural production any more. Those who will view feature length films in the darkened social space of the cinema, with its implications on creating a public, must be counted in the minority. And if so, the functioning or breakdown of technology (see Larkin, 2004), the poor quality of DVDs, VCDs and downloaded versions of films, and the cramped spaces of computer and television monitors must all be considered.

By 'globalisation', then, to take this a step further and to localise it to Morocco, I mean a period of time and a set of cultural concerns in Morocco and Moroccan art and literature that succeeds that which we call the postcolonial period, even while many of the obsessions and anxieties of the postcolonial still are present. This transition to the 'age of circulation' and this tension with respect to the postcolonial period can be felt from the start of our appreciation of the controversies around *Marock* announced at the outset: the anxiety over the French provenance of, funding for and diasporic location of the director of the film (postcolonial considerations) vs. the Hollywood 'look', global 'morals' and cybermediated/cyberfacilitated discussions of the film (we will see these echoed within the film later). Films such as *Marock, Baidaoua* (dir. Abdelkader Lagtaa, 1999), *Ali Zaoua* (dir. Nabil Ayouch, 2000), *Khahit errouh/Threads* (dir. Hakim Belabbes, 2003), and *Le Grand voyage* (dir. Ismael Ferroukhi, 2004), which in various ways engage the question of the state of the Moroccan nation (the last two explicitly through the lens of diaspora), do not do so burdened by the anxieties of carving out an independent, postcolonial nation free from the pull of French culture and epistemologies. Rather, they are concerned with what place Morocco and Moroccan culture might have in a global setting within which ideas, products and commodities, lifestyles and technologies have complicated what was once, perhaps, a more binary situation. I say this without meaning to reduce colonial (and postcolonial) Morocco to a binary, either internally, with respect to French division of Arab and Tamazight cultures/languages/populations, or globally, with respect to the changing position of the US toward Morocco (and Morocco toward the US) in the late colonial and first two decades of the postcolonial period. As I have argued elsewhere, from the arrival of American troops in Morocco in November 1942, and certainly after Franklin Roosevelt's participation in the Casablanca Conference in January 1943, there was a vivid and visible triangulation of paradigms available in Morocco, within which the American position might offer liberty from the French; the promise/threat of American commodities was the harbinger of this new paradigm.[6] To say so is not to confuse the American 'alternative' as liberating, though that was the terms within which Roosevelt spoke to Mohammed V, but rather with a postcolonial arrangement which would threaten to place Morocco in the time lag of American neoliberalism *avant la lettre*. But even if we agree that the postcolonial period be reconsidered itself outside the terms of binarisms, we still will note the shift, with the 1970s, into a new set of concerns and ways of engaging with social collectivities in Morocco.

In geopolitical terms, attending to an episteme associated with globalisation is to account for the changes in the world order after a variety of demarcations: 1973 (the shift off the gold standard, end of major fighting in Vietnam, waning of *années de plomb* period in Morocco, end of student unrest of the late 1960s in Morocco; see

Tessler, 1993); 1991 (end of the cold war, dissolution of USSR, US war in Iraq); 2001 (11 September attacks, US war in Afghanistan); 2003 (US invasion of Iraq, bombings in Casablanca). These are markers that matter particularly in the realm of national and global politics. Cohen and Jaidi, in their consideration of globalisation and its effects on Moroccan politics and economy, designate the period from the mid-1970s until 1996 as one of semi-liberalisation, a period that begins when the contest over the monarch's power and place in Moroccan governance is finally accepted (after the harsh repressions of the *années de plomb*), and a combination of scepticism, apoliticism, self-censorship and mobilisation 'from outside'. The political unrest that builds through the 1980s into the early 1990s, with a series of large and sometimes violent demonstrations, may be seen to lead to the arrival of the government of 'alternance', or the coming to power of the opposition party in 1997 (coincidentally, the year when *Marock* is set). In the terms that matter particularly to the analysis of film and literature, it is also to recognise that the conditions within which such forms of artistic production operate now include other dramatically space–time collapsing technologies such as satellite TV, fax machines, mobile telephones (and forms of textual production such as TXT messaging that emerged alongside them) and the Internet, all of which had positive effects on the loosening of political censorship and opening of political communication with the outside.

I do not see these geopological and cultural-technological shifts as separate or even as separable. This is something that Moroccan films such as *Marock, Baidaoua, Le Grand voyage*, *Threads* and *Ali Zaoua* make vivid, all in markedly different ways. *Marock*, made in 2005, is set in 1997, and thus sensitive to the moment before cell phones and the Internet pervaded daily life in Morocco, but no less attentive to the new circulation of cultural objects in its setting, and acutely aware of the use of new technologies to market the film. *Baidaoua*, with its interest in circulation, censorship and morality police (who represent the lack of free circulation), is less interested in technology and more in immobility in time and space as a challenge to contemporary Morocco—the contrast between the feminist protagonist Salwa's desire to get a restricted book, which may require her to leave the country, and the Islamist teacher's comments that the Koran is good for all times and places suggests the ways in which circulation is associated with temporality and stasis. *Le Grand voyage*, a road movie from Paris to Mecca, portrays the cell phone in connection with travel, as a technology that challenges the authority of face to face contact, and also symbolises the generational gap. Hakim Belabbes's *Khahit errouh/Threads*, an experimental, avant-garde film, associates the ruptures of generational and diasporic change, of its shift in setting from Chicago to Boujjad, and perhaps of its own avant-garde fragmented technique with the interruption of the telephone, a technology of connection that ruptures. And *Ali Zaoua* demonstrates in two ways a sense that the world of young street children may be seen in relationship to the technologies and economic forces of globalisation: its framing device of mass media attention to the subculture the film itself represents and its creative use of digitally generated animation to depict the imaginary of these children. By forwarding these concerns, I do not mean to suggest that these are the only interesting things going on in the films, nor to suggest that the primary consideration in them—with the exception of *Le Grand voyage*—is not the nation itself. *Le Grand voyage* is a film about diaspora and movement, even if it can also be read as a film about the transition between generations of Maghribis as they move into diaspora.

Yet even narratives that are centred around the nation, or a critique of the nation, must be considered in the changed framework within which the nation operates within globalisation.[7] For *Marock*, sensitive to the global movement of ideas, images, bodies and commodities (to say nothing of politics and technologies), awareness of this framework is crucial to judging the film and whether Marrakchi's national critique is anachronistic, daring, or both. In *Baidaoua*, awareness of this context allows us to see how the film is concerned primarily with circulation, whether or not one can move socially, across borders, within a city. In *Ali Zaoua*, taking this in another direction, social immobility is contrasted with the mobilities represented by media and digital animation. Shifting the conversation to 'circulation' is partially to register frustration with a logic that insists that all Moroccan cultural production after 1956 forever after is in reference to France, and to insist that other concerns and other networks do in fact take centre stage in recent years.[8] *Marock*'s intertwined set of concerns include questions of circulation, diaspora, cultural clash, friction with (or rupture from) Moroccan traditions, together which suggest that the analytics of 'postcolonialism' do not here apply, *even though* postcolonialism may be the register within which Marrakchi imagines the narrative resolution of her film via Rita's departure from Morocco to France, which I will associate with the film's anachronism below. I am not the first critic to suggest that the postcolonial period (and more provocatively postcolonial theory itself) be considered a temporal stage that has been succeeded by something else.[9] Given that 'globalisation' is still in danger of being misread, and given the importance of the intertwined movements of commodities, bodies and finances suggested above, I use 'age of circulation' as synonymous. Also, 'circulation' will open up a way of reading the text and the conditions for its movement that will prove useful in understanding both how *Marock* works and what it shares with other recent Moroccan films and cultural products, even those that take different positions with respect to domestic Morocco, diaspora and emigration.

To focus on the stage of 'globalisation' will mean to attend to a different sort of engagement with the US and American culture, and *Marock* is notable for the way in which American objects, songs, and what I called above a Hollywood 'look' run through a film that otherwise is not geographically concerned with the United States. Here we have perhaps our clearest explanation for how what I'm calling the 'age of circulation' follows the concerns of the 'postcolonial' period. If the cultural concerns of postcolonial Maghribi cultural production revolve around an anxious relationship to French history, culture and language—perhaps the pinnacle in Morocco is Abdelkebir Khatibi's novel *La Mémoire tatouée* (1971) or in historiography Abdellah Laroui's *L'histoire du Maghreb* (1970)—in the cultural production of what I am calling the age of circulation, or globalisation, the concerns are different. Perhaps it is not coincidental that in recent cinema we see this engagement most visibly, or most centrally, and earlier (for example, Abdelkader Lagtaa's 1991 film *al-Hubb fi al-Dar al-Baida*; see Edwards, 2003), for even within the colonial period, American cinematic representations of Morocco (such as *Casablanca*) were a harbinger of the later geopolitical order that would follow the colonial era. But we do see this interest in circulation in recent Moroccan literature (e.g. Aicha Ech-Chana's socially committed documentary text *Miseria*, 1996, and Soumya Zahy's 2001 novel *On ne rentrera peut-être plus jamais chez nous*), and less surprisingly in literature of the Moroccan diaspora, such as Abdelkader Benali, writing in Holland (in Dutch), Laila Lalami, writing in the US (in English), both of whom narrate tales of Moroccans in motion to and from Europe.

What I am interested by in *Marock*, then, is less the film as aesthetically pleasing or narratively original. In these categories, it disappoints. It does after all look much like a 'teen picture', or familiar romantic tragedy. Lagtaa's *Baidaoua*, which summons an innovative visual technique in the service of a complex narrative exploration of circulation, is significantly more original from an aesthetic point of view (see Edwards, 2005b). But *Marock* is nonetheless successful in making clear the forms of social organisation produced by and within the 'age of circulation'. My contention is that a careful reading of the film will help us derive those concerns in the Moroccan case.

Reading Marock

In its coverage of the debate over *Marock*, the maverick weekly *Le Journal Hebdomadaire* staged a debate between Bilal Talidi, a representative of the Islamist PJD (Parti de la justice et du développement), which had called for banning the film, and Abdellah Zaazaa, the leader of a network of Casablanca neighbourhood associations called RESAQ (Réseau des Associations de Quartier du Grand Casablanca) and representative of a liberal, secular position (Houdaifa and Tounassi, 2006). In the debate, printed in the pages of *Le Journal*, the question of aesthetics became a screen against which to debate larger questions about Moroccan society. Talidi, who had published an editorial against *Marock* in the paper *Attajdid*, claimed in the pages of *Le Journal* that 'one should not judge a film without watching it'. His indictment of the film was, in this venue, pitched in terms of aesthetic reasons: a 'maladroit' use of French and Arabic, an 'extreme lightness of plot' and a lack of 'dynamism, drama or life'; for him, it was closer to a documentary than a 'true film'. Zaazaa, on the other hand, resisted the analysis of the film's language or aesthetic quality and launched his own defence on political grounds. The film's ability to 'trace Moroccan realities', in particular, justified its screening in Morocco, and he called attention to the ways in which its opposition was manipulating the film for its ulterior motives of creating a 'State of law' (*Etat de droit*). But he too made recourse to aesthetic judgment. He notes: 'I saw the film in the company of my wife. We left struck [*boulversés*] by how well it had traced Moroccan social realities. The story pleased me in every way.' The point that he had seen the film in the company of his wife, clearly, was part of his implied defence. If *Marock* posed a challenge to 'traditions of the country', 'religious values' and the 'fundamentals of Islam' (as other religious politicians had suggested, including those who did not call for its censorship, but rather for a national boycott; Houdaifa and Tounassi, 2006, pp. 20–1), Zaazaa claimed that the film could educate the Moroccan conjugal couple on the new realities of Moroccan society. Still, Talidi called Zaazaa on the latter's expression of 'pleasure' on seeing the film, which the former said was not an 'objective response', and therefore to be discarded. Talidi claimed such objectivity for his own analysis of the film; Zaazaa's pleasure was seen as subjective.

Marock, the viewing of *Marock*, the response one had to the viewing of *Marock*, and what the nation's appropriate response to *Marock* should be, became in 2006 fraught places to debate the status of national culture itself. Talidi's comment about Zaazaa's pleasure begs the question of an 'objective' reading. How do we read this film? How do we avoid the trap of reading for 'meaning'? And can an 'objective' reading of the film by a representative of a political party stand in for that of a citizenry?

Talidi and Zaazaa notably agreed that *Marock* offered a representation of Moroccan reality, though they did not call attention to their agreement on this question. For

Talidi, *Marock* was more documentary than film; for Zaazaa, it was a shocking representation of a reality he recognised, but about which he did not know before. Their implied disagreement is over what role the elite and Westward-looking Moroccan youth of *Marock* might have in society at large. As we will see, it is the very 'teen' look of the picture, inscribed within a style deeply redolent of American cinema, that is perhaps the most upsetting, though these were not the terms used in the debate. PJD's call for the film to be banned drew on the law's defence of 'sacred values and good morals'. Therefore, the question of whether the film was Moroccan or not could be linked to whether it should be banned under Moroccan law. Marrakchi's Moroccanness or her Frenchness was itself a cipher for a question of *style* and what I call the film's 'look'. A closer examination will show how *Marock* itself exhibits, on the level of style, the circulation of an American look doubled by the film's interest in (both visually and in the scenario) American commodities. This is the threat that is harder to speak of, but the one which makes the PJD position ultimately anachronistic, as other commentators realised. Mohamed Ameskane, representative of UMP, stated in the same pages that the film could be boycotted, 'if it was judged contrary to our principles. [But] one must sign up for this new world, the world of the Internet and of globalisation.' Seen in this light, the resistance to *Marock* by many Moroccan commentators should be seen as aligned with an anxiety about globalisation, and the championing of it on grounds of 'free speech' can be seen as a celebration of the open borders (of both information and trade in commodities) associated with globalisation. My point is not to take a side, but to show that *Marock* heralds, but does not initiate, a new stage in Moroccan cinema. From *Marock*, we'll be able to look backward to see this interest in circulation in a number of places. But first we must describe how a 'look' circulates.

The story *Marock* tells is familiar enough to those who have watched Hollywood teen romances, and on the level of plot it borrows from a number of Hollywood films and TV serials. To say so is not to denigrate it, *per se*—though neither is it a compliment on artistic grounds—but rather to note why the familiarity of the formula could itself be so bothersome to some Moroccan critics such as Talidi, and also why for others it immediately raised the question of protection on the grounds of free speech. What I will call the 'circulation' of this look operates on both the level of plot/scenario (which allowed politicians to target the film) and the visual and aural registers of the film (that which politicians did not invoke). *Marock* borrows what we can call, following Miriam Hansen, a 'vernacular' familiar from Hollywood cinema, in this case the teen romance, and brings it into Moroccan circulation. That combination of a familiar 'look' and the familiarity of the Hollywood formula of the 'problem' picture-cum-teen romance will emerge as the most interesting form of global culture in circulation in this film. But we will also note the many explicit indications of global circulation: the music, apparel, food, products and commodities that animate the world of these Casablancan youth. If these youth look to Europe for their futures after the *bac*, the commodities, products, and culture that they consume are for the most part American. More accurately, these objects of consumption are 'global', and generally rendered in 'global English', both of which are associated with the US irrespective of the national origin of the cultural product or artist.

Marock is a 'teen pic', which seems at once a comfortable and uncomfortable phrase to describe it, given that the phrase implies an American relationship to the family and society that is not the norm in Morocco. From the evidence of *Marock*, however, not only does 'teen pic' sound appropriate to describe the film, but the film so successfully mobilises this style to describe a social milieu that it effaces for its non-Moroccan audiences much of the particularity of Moroccan adolescence. Such particularity is swept away by *Marock*'s depiction of a world of discos, parties, romance and preparation for a life after high school that will be spent in France. Whatever the accuracy of this representation of the young elite of Casablanca, it is clearly not the life enjoyed by most Moroccans. (As a pedagogical strategy, juxtaposing *Ali Zaoua*, with its representation of the poor homeless children of Casablanca, and *Marock*, the two Moroccan films of the first decade of the twenty-first century with the largest international success, would be provocative.) With poverty and social class for the most part dispensed with by *Marock*'s fascination with the elite, the 'problems' that remain in the 'social problem' aspects of the film are those presented by Moroccan society itself. Perhaps, then, it is not surprising that the solutions to those problems are also brought in from abroad (American music, for example, and the characters' choice to depart from Morocco). The way what I will call the film's Hollywood 'look' functions, then, is to naturalise the import of foreign solutions to domestic problems, and to make domestic recalcitrance to them seem itself foreign or anachronistic. That is, the film's adoption of an American vernacular, within which the social problem of a romance between a Jewish young man and a Muslim young woman may be overcome naturally by the power of love (and romantic comedy as a genre), was a solution that made its own difficulty to imagine for most Moroccans seem irrelevant or retrograde. Indeed, the film ends in tragedy with respect to the love story, not the comedy it has suggested, which we may see as the translation of the vernacular to local 'realities'. This relationship to the Hollywood vernacular is the deep level on which Marrakchi's outsider perspective functions, and though unnamed by its opponents, it produced the relationship to Morocco that many found bothersome about the film—and which titillated others. But without the language to discuss this vernacular as that which was foreign to the Moroccan film, the debate revolved instead around the question of Marrakchi's roots as a Moroccan or the route she took to France as ways to prove that she and therefore her film were not after all 'Moroccan'. This, it should be clear, was a dead-end.

The story is a simple problem tale set during the month of Ramadan. Rita is a high school senior; it is the year of the baccalaureate exam, a year that in her circles is spent studying, partying, listening to music, and thinking about the next stage of life. For Rita and most of her friends at the privileged Lycée Lyautey, the next stage of life often means leaving Morocco for Europe (though not for all); the present is generally met with abandon. Drinking alcohol, smoking hashish, flirtations, and a fair amount of sexual activity are the norm for weekend nights, which are spent racing around in sports cars between nightclubs and homes without parents, where prostitutes may be called in for quick fixes for the boys. Rita's brother Mao has returned home from London for Ramadan, and from the start we can see that he does not approve of the milieu. We see Mao praying, to the surprise of his sister, and wearing a close cropped beard; he is clearly disturbed by the frivolities of his old circle of friends. He rarely comments directly, except to Rita, whom he says looks like a 'whore' because of her makeup. At a party, Rita falls for a young man she has observed at a nightclub. She learns his name (Youri) through a mutual friend, and bets her friends that she'll have him by the end of Ramadan. The problem, though, is not whether she can or will have him—there are meaningful glances between them from the start that make this clear—but what it will mean if she does have him. Youri is after all a Moroccan Jew, and while this seems to bother no one too much in the present (except Mao, who is teased by friends and reports it to his parents), the fact that these young people's future always is on their minds poses the question that Rita rarely asks herself. Can this relationship have a future? Learning about Rita's social life from Mao, Rita's parents ground her until the *bac* is over and done with. Still she escapes, consummates her affair with Youri, passes her *bac*, and worries about what to do with her romance if it cannot be shared openly. She suggests to Youri that he could convert to Islam; he suggests the same to her about Judaism. No sooner has this been discussed than Youri kills himself in a car crash. Rita, distraught, retreats into herself. Her brother apologises for his part in her unhappiness. They reconcile. Two months pass. Rita leaves for Europe.

The plot is fast and efficient. The film is visually sensuous; its world is socially vapid. Rita, played by a newcomer to the cinema that Marrakchi plucked from Paris and who admitted in interviews to being from the same elevated Casablanca class that is depicted in the film, is attractive and starry eyed. (Morjana Alaoui was in fact a student at the American University in Paris when Marrakchi cast her in her first film role; after passing her *bac* in Morocco, she had lived in Florida. Her own pathways neatly demonstrate the triangulation of colonial/postcolonial and global that I have discussed above.) She is also barely clad much of the time, in close fitting tank tops and boxer shorts, in a string bikini another time, or faded Levis, costuming choices that are both part of the film's verisimilitude in representing the young Casa elite—from press photos and in film festival appearances, it is striking how much Marrakchi herself looks like and dresses like her own characters[10]—and part of Marrakchi's juxtaposition of the visual appearances of the libertine Casablancan youth and the more traditional members of the community. The most famous example of this juxtaposition appeared in the film still circulated as part of the film's publicity and which appeared on the cover of *Tel Quel*. In the still, Rita wears skin-tight shorts and a cotton camisole, hand on hip, navel exposed, and stands over her brother at prayer. In the film's scene, she provokes him: 'Are you sick or what? What are you doing? Did you fall on your head?' Then, more aggressively: 'Do you think you're in Algeria? Are you going to become a fundamentalist (*barbu*)?' The pose, reproduced on the cover of *Tel Quel* next to the words 'the film of all taboos' (my translation), presents a vivid example of the changing look of young women in Casablanca, not only in terms of clothing and brands, but in body size and type itself. During the period when *Marock* is set, in the late 1990s, sociologist Fatima Mernissi was writing columns in the Casablanca-based women's magazine *Femmes du Maroc* that remarked on the generational shift of young Moroccan women increasingly toward western body types as models of beauty; this was a shift Mernissi lamented as she called for Moroccan women to resist the emaciated 'waif' look of then prominent models such as Kate Moss (see Mernissi, 1998).

Mernissi's comments on the ways in which Moroccan women's body types could represent a form of cultural circulation, along with Susan Ossman's subsequent ethnographic work that charted the transnational circulation of western models of beauty and body type, open up the ways in which we can discuss the western 'look' of the film, both in terms of the individual actors, their bodies and clothing, and the cinematic vernacular that Marrakchi mobilises. It is after all the 'look' thus conceived that is the most immediate presence of America in a film that only once invokes the US as a geopolitical entity (and then quickly dispenses with it as a place where the characters know 'no one', as we'll see). Still America plays a major, if imagined and silent, presence in the film. In so doing, *Marock* presents itself to us as a film that is not postcolonial but rather one that inhabits the 'age of circulation' in an interrelated series of ways. Before we come back to the literal markers of this presence of global culture, let us attempt to describe the more slippery question of what I've referred to as the film's Hollywood teen pic vernacular.

Miriam Hansen has in several recent essays presented a powerful argument that broadens our understanding of what she calls the 'vexed issue of Americanism' for transnational cinema studies, namely, the ways in which 'an aesthetic idiom developed in one country could achieve transnational and global currency' (1999, p. 60). Her focus has been on the circulation of the 'classical' style of Hollywood cinema, namely, the narrative cinema produced during the dominance of the studio system (roughly 1917–60), and the ways in which that style has been translated and differently understood in a variety of other national cinemas—most notably, in her own work, Shanghai cinema. There are at least two lessons from Hansen's rich work that I want to bring in here. First is her analysis of the way in which classical narrative Hollywood cinema masks the 'anachronistic tension' of its 'combination of neoclassicist style and Fordist mass culture' (p. 66). The anachronism of classical cinema is that it takes on neoclassicist aesthetics (it is readerly, transparent, has linear narratives, coherent subjects, etc.) even while it was an art associated with the 'new' and the 'modern', both as a new technology and with respect to the Fordist mass (cultural) production perfected by the studio system. By naturalising its own form of narrative, Hansen argues, classical Hollywood cinema developed a rhetoric that could in fact articulate 'something radically new and different under the guise of a continuity with tradition' (p. 67). Part of what is articulated is the very messiness of Fordism and modernity itself, with its various forms of structural and literal violence and how (certain) individuals could find a place in that system. Hansen's second lesson, then, follows from this first one, and is related to our discussion of circulation. Namely, that Hollywood cinema travelled so well, and so much better than other national cinemas, because of the way it 'forg[ed] a mass market out of an ethnically and cultural heterogeneous society, if often at the expense of racial others' (p. 68). This—the 'first global vernacular'—worked because classical Hollywood cinema mobilised 'biologically hardwired structures and universal narrative templates'; mediated competing discourses on modernity and modernisation; and because 'it articulated, multiplied, and globalized a particular historical experience' (p. 68). Much of the way Hollywood cinema found its way influentially into other national cinemas was not because classical cinema universalised the American experience, but rather because it was translatable. '[I]t meant different things to different publics, both at home and abroad', Hansen writes (p. 68). On the level of reception, the Hollywood films, followed by that which might be taken from them (their rhetoric), could be changed, localised and adapted.

Hansen's work is generative. What I want to borrow here, at the risk of playing too loosely with the historical categories Hansen is discussing, is her discussion of the contradictions that the classical style masks and allows, and her sense of how that particular conjunction itself is particularly well suited for global circulation. This allows us to revisit the discussion of 'cultures of circulation' that Lee and LiPuma advance and to balance the temptation to read for meaning with an attention to what Gaonkar and Povinelli called the 'circulatory matrix'. *Marock*'s engagement with a Hollywood 'vernacular'—no longer the classical vernacular, pure and simple, though at most times borrowing from it—allows it to smooth over some of the more troubling aspects of economic globalisation that affect the world behind that which is represented in the film. The film does attend to class and economic differences repeatedly, even while too comfortably keeping them at the margins. But this smoothing over of the crises of economic globalisation happens naturally, as it were, in the fluid way in which *Marock* adopts the cultural style or look of the Hollywood teen pic. In other words, the ways in which the film may be seen in terms of 'globalisation' are multiple and reinforce one another: the circulation of the Hollywood vernacular and the fascination with American cultural products and commodities serve both to double the elite characters' ability to circulate across national borders and to efface the ways in which the Moroccan underclass may not. When Rita's friend Asmaa (Razika Simozrag) tells Mao that she will not be relocating to Europe after the *bac* because her parents don't have the means, he does not know what to say. Mao's surprise—'je savais pas', he mutters and looks down—is echoed, as it were, by the film's inability to dwell on those who do not circulate. Though the film notes these individuals who represent dead-ends, it cannot itself resist always remaining in motion.

Marock, to be clear, is most fascinated by upper middle class teenagers in Casablanca, a group whose own ability to circulate is strikingly more capacious than other Moroccans. This is a point the film does suggest, particularly vividly in a climactic scene when Rita denounces her parents for paying off the family of a young poor child whom Mao apparently struck with his car and killed at some time in the past. And while the film does offer sympathetic portraits of working class Moroccans as minor figures (most often as servants, by which it offers an additional critique of upper middle class Moroccan family values), its portrait of Morocco is clearly delimited to a small portion of the population. That it did apparently speak to a much larger public than that it represented, though, should not be doubted, in part perhaps because of the film's own subtle critique of class dynamics, but otherwise because of the apparent translatability of some of the aspirations of its characters to other social classes among Moroccan youth. Still, the visual pleasure the film takes in depicting sumptuous residences, cars, parties and bodies of Casablanca's elite ally it with the Hollywood 'teen picture' and not with class critique. To be sure, *Marock* is not a critique of globalisation, either economic or cultural.

The immediacy and power of the Moroccan debate around *Marock* with which I began this discussion, then, can be seen as the resistance of Moroccans left behind by those very processes of globalisation, both cultural and economic, which Marrakchi's film represents and enacts. Hansen's crucial point that the classical style was anachronistic—because neoclassical and modern, which I might recast as 'preposterous', meaning simultaneously 'before' and 'after' (see Edwards, 2003)—may be borrowed with respect to Marrakchi's translation of the Hollywood 'teen pic'. In this sense, *Marock* is a film that struck many Moroccan viewers as new (Zaazaa's comments in Houdaifa and Tounassi, 2006), and yet it is a film that is clearly nostalgic for a different form of looking at and being in the world, a world before the advent of digital technologies. *Marock*, with its familiar soundtrack of rock and roll, dance club and disco hits, offers then the newness of a 'modern' Morocco, engaging the putatively taboo topics of teen sexuality and interreligious relationships, along with a reassuringly retro soundtrack—some of the songs featured most prominently are Snap!, 'The Power' (1990); David Bowie, 'Rock 'n' Roll Suicide' (1972); Peaches and Herb, 'Shake Your Groove Thing' (1978); Ronnie Bird, 'Sad Soul' (1969); and The Auteurs, 'Junk Shop Clothes' (1993). It is that 'retro' soundtrack that hints at the retrograde anachronism of Marrakchi's resolution of her tale. The nostalgia for a world before digital technologies overwhelmed daily practice substitutes or overlays smoothly, as I've suggested, an allegory of the Moroccan nation for the more complex situation of contemporary Morocco in the age of circulation. That is, the way in which *Marock* proposes itself as something radically new on the Moroccan cultural scene and then delivers in multiple ways something more comfortably nostalgic is the way in which its look and soundtrack betray the trap that the film slips into: the idea that national allegory provides an adequate mode within which to comprehend twenty-first century Moroccan reality.

In *Marock*, the interplay of new and nostalgic is associated throughout with the Hollywood look. The camera savours the streets, exteriors and interiors of the wealthy Anfa neighbourhood of Casablanca, to a slow sensual rock and roll soundtrack. Even to those who have been to privileged neighbourhoods of Casablanca and Rabat, the scenes depict an almost impossibly wealthy milieu. *Marock* includes several scenes that do nothing to advance the plot but which are nonetheless crucial to comprehending its meaning: a car chase through the streets of Anfa, several scenes of the young characters sitting around swimming pools, nightclubs, and outdoor cafés. They curse, they drink alcohol, the young men harass the female maids. The film's global audience and its Moroccan audience alike are in a familiar world, but one not familiar from film images of Morocco in general or Casablanca in particular. It is a world familiar from TV and Hollywood images of Beverly Hills. The language of the film is for the most part French (only the servants speak in Moroccan Arabic), a choice that Marrakchi defended on the grounds of realism (Antona, 2006). If this is more 'real' a representation of the bourgeoisie, it also comes in the look of a foreign film, and that is precisely the point. Antona, a French interviewer, asked if the (limited) amount of Arabic used in the film would limit the film's 'accessibility', presumably to French audiences. If to some younger Moroccan audiences the film brought together a Hollywood look with Moroccan actors and backgrounds, to the French interviewer the global circulation worked in a different direction—the difference of Moroccan Arabic stood out.

What the exchange between Antona and Marrakchi reveals, almost painfully, is how Marrakchi's choice to write out Moroccan Arabic and with it the bulk of the Moroccan population (save the elite of Casablanca) follows the directives of globalisation as form of economic distribution. This silent translation of Moroccan Arabic is the flattening of language so that it might circulate more easily, the reduction of local/national particularity to global 'value' (see Judy, 1997; see also Spivak, 2003). By claiming that her choice to render so much of her film in French was based on realism, Marrakchi not only reveals the partial nature of her regard of contemporary Morocco but also demonstrates her intention that her film *stand in* for the Moroccan nation. The moments in *Marock* that gesture toward those who are left out of its perspective are thereby deleted (or put in parentheses), as with a keystroke, as illegible and thereby irrelevant.

That the film imagines itself as an allegory of the nation itself is clear from its title, which plays on the French name for Morocco, adding a 'k' to suggest contemporaneity via the reference to rock music. Organising its narrative around the coming-of-age of its protagonist as she comes up against the recalcitrance of her own society invokes a well-worn formula. But if *Marock* claims contemporaneity, it is unable to offer more than a repetition of that oldest of postcolonial narrative resolutions: the departure from the nation that cannot contain the enlightened consciousness of the protagonist. This resolution, however, exceeds the cultural conditions of the moment being represented, in that departure and travel itself do not have the status they once did—particularly not for Rita's class. Departure from Morocco, therefore, cannot equal renunciation or enlightenment without eliminating the very contemporaneity that the film wants to claim. The import of what I consider an anachronistic formula to resolve the film narrative suggests how important nostalgia is for Marrakchi in the attempt to efface that anachronism (or the audience's awareness of it). Further, it suggests why the category of 'circulation', which is the obsession of the film, is a contested one. Not surprisingly, 'circulation' operates or signifies multiply within the film.

Contested interpretations of 'circulation' within *Marock*—those uses which Marrakchi makes of it, on the one hand, and how I think it offers an analytic tool by which to suggest the anachronistic limits of her project in national allegory, on the other—demonstrate Hansen's point about the way in which global vernaculars can mean different things to different audiences. As a way to further elaborate this point and to move toward a conclusion of this analysis of the film's relationship to circulation, the car race scene is perhaps worth a second look, precisely because it is so formulaic and unoriginal. There is little apparent importance to the scene, other than that it appears in a Moroccan film at all. Youri has Rita in his car and races two other cars driven by his buddies, each of which is stocked with a young woman in the passenger seat. Youri of course wins the race because of his daring, cutting down a side street recklessly; that he will eventually die in a car crash is clearly signalled. The scene's very banality makes it interesting for our purposes: it is literally about circulation in two ways that French language makes possible. First, there are no cars on the streets of Anfa, presumably cleared by Marrakchi and her crew; as an audience we never fear that a car will appear out of nowhere. We are in a pure space of cinema. The cars may circulate without traffic. Second, the Hollywood B-movie staple is here represented in a Moroccan film. It is not the first car chase in a Moroccan film, surely, but it is one that signals the *circulation* of the Hollywood vernacular (of the 'teen pic', of the banal movie, of the picture in which 'true love', forged between a young man and a young woman across the space of a passenger car, can cure all social ills).

Indeed, in its very familiarity from Hollywood films, *Marock*'s car race scene evokes an earlier scene in the film in which the fact that the free circulation of automobiles is inhibited allows for romance. If the car race seems to invoke Hollywood, the earlier scene invokes Morocco in its attention to social details, or at least the Morocco of the *haute bourgeoisie*. What happens is this: Rita is being driven home from school by the family chauffeur when they come across Youri's car and his family's driver, broken down at the side of the road. Rita (or rather her driver) offers Youri a ride home, which allows the couple to make eyes at one another and begin their romance. This scene works within the teen pic vernacular, but it also localises it to its own particular class/national location. That Youri's car is not in circulation, suffering a moment of Moroccan technological breakdown (see Larkin, 2004), should be juxtaposed with the rapid and easy circulation in the car race scene, an easy adaptation of the Hollywood vernacular; it is what I call an 'end of circulation'. The fact that this scene allows Rita and Youri to enjoy the later car scene (the race) in which their love is symbolically consummated (as it will be sexually consummated later), will in turn produce a second Moroccan response that forces a temporary end to circulation. Namely, that Rita, found out by her parents, will be enclosed in her own enormous house. Her own social circulation is cut off, at least for a moment until her bac is passed when she may continue her circulatory trajectory toward Europe. The car chase, banal and not visually compelling, thus can be understood as the key to the ways in which circulation operates multiply in *Marock*.

If driving around in cars—racing, being driven to and from school, drinking and driving—is an important component of the film's grammar, *Marock*'s obsession with the circulation of commodities provides the conjunctions to those sentences. In the world of *Marock*, pirated Hollywood films get delivered to your driveway by video rental agents with their inventory in the trunk of their car and friends from Miami send you authentic New York Yankee caps (to pick two details that are given attention within the film). These products not only lubricate the social relations of the characters' interactions, but they sometimes provide the film with spoken or visual words that echo the cinematic vernacular I have discussed. Words, products, and phrases on t-shirts may be seen to offer further ver-isimilitude in Marrakchi's representation of her milieu. But they eventually jump right off the page. My eye is drawn to the American t-shirts running through *Marock*. 'Hopper for State Senate' reads one that Youri wears; 'Where in the Hell is Slippery Rock' reads another. Why wear such particular phrases? Are they markers of distinction, like Driss's (Rachid Benhaissan) cherished NY Yankee cap, tossed around the swimming pool away from its owner's grasp? Our eyes are drawn to English language phrases on the characters' clothing, clothing which may or may not be authentic imports, just as the detached signifier of American phrases (often with spelling or grammatical errors) appears on clothing for sale throughout Moroccan cities today.

For the bulk of the film, these phrases and the commodities they decorate serve merely to echo and solidify the theme of circulation I have identified. But in one of the final scenes of the film, there is a twist. Youri's death in a car crash, though appar-ently accidental, occurs shortly after Rita and he have discussed their society's unwill-ingness to admit an affair between a Moroccan Jew and Moroccan Muslim. Mao is the character who most assumes the guilt of this societal intractability, since it is he who had informed his parents about Rita's affair and he who seems most disturbed by the affair (also, symbolically, since Mao had struck and killed a boy with his car before the action of the film, and the compensation for this killing has not been yet satisfied). After Youri's death, we are forced to watch the impossibly painful melodrama of a high school girl mourning the death of her boyfriend. There is nothing that can be said, and the film is silent—without words. Silent that is until Mao comes up to Rita's rooftop perch and reconciles with her. When he arrives, he is wearing a t-shirt printed with the word 'America', a small heart dotting the 'i'. There is no justification in the plot for his shirt (Mao supposedly lives in London), and it is unlike anything he has worn before. In fact, it seems impossible to imagine the character Mao wearing this shirt. But his shirt, which speaks before he does, suggests something about the depth of the apology he is making and underlines his implied renunciation of the intolerance he showed earlier toward Youri's religion.

The suggestion this t-shirt makes is complex. Given the association in Morocco and throughout the Muslim world of the US with support for Israel, wearing the 'America' shirt here presents a layered message. The America of the cultural products and film ver-nacular is now the America that loves the departed Youri, and the liberal sentiment toward tolerance and inclusion that the film is offering as its solution to the film's problem. It is important to note that America is not a place that the characters imagine going to lit-erally—it is mentioned once, as a place not possible. Rita had asked Youri what he will do after passing the *bac*. He says that his parents want to go to America, but he knows *'personne'* (no one). The nobody that he knows is modulated by his parents' suggestion that America is the place where they, as Moroccan Jews, will go to after he graduates high school. The potential of Youri's circulation in America is named by Mao's shirt, but of course Youri will not circulate in America because he will be dead. Thus the t-shirt initiates its own conversation about the possibility or impossibility of Moroccans to circulate along the multiple registers I have been naming.

The appearance of the startling t-shirt here demonstrates how Marrakchi associates the circulation of commodities with her own national allegory. 'America' appears on the t-shirt to signify the tolerance that the film argues Morocco does not have but should learn to have. The t-shirt also suggests how Marrakchi anachronistically combines the national allegory form and the resolution she arrives at for her allegory (departure) to grapple with a Morocco already within the grip of globalisation, as represented here by the t-shirt, the last of the global commodities to make a cameo appearance. The Morocco that she represents in *Marock*, that is to say, is already within what I have called the 'age of circulation' within which national allegory must be insufficient. Thus, despite the fact that Rita is in tears when Mao (wearing 'America') embraces her, the fact that her friends are in tears as she leaves Morocco for France, and that the price for both scenes is the death of Youri, the film makes it possible to see Rita's departure for France and reconciliation with her brother as a particular form of comic resolution. This should be disturbing. Indeed, *Tel Quel* called it a 'happy end', using the American expression, and claimed that this reconciliation between siblings without religious conversion was the final 'taboo' the film had broken (Boukhari, 2006). Since *Tel Quel* was one of *Marock*'s greatest champions precisely on the basis of the film's willingness to challenge Moroccan taboos, the ease with which the magazine's editors might slip into the epistemological trap of falling for Marrakchi's national allegory may be explained, yet again, by the peculiar seduction of the film's vernacular.

Envoi

As *Marock* circulated from Paris to Cannes, and from Tangier to Casablanca to the streets of Fez, where I bought my pirated copy on the sidewalks of the *ville nouvelle*, it was following yet another trajectory than the one it depicts. (I later bought a legal copy of the film, which is currently distributed in Canada and France.) The trajectory of the film's circulation in 2006 was much more complex than the social world represented by a young woman taking an airplane from a Casablanca that has disappointed her to a Paris that offers her escape. Discussions of the film raged on the Internet, in blogs and chatrooms, from 'bladi.net' to Islamist sites (where Marrakchi's alleged support of Danish newspapers publishing cartoons depicting the Prophet was marshalled against her in one strand of discussion). The space in time from 1997, the fictional world of *Marock*, to 2005 when it was made, was immense. And to imagine a social world of elite young Moroccans that did not involve mobile telephones, TXT messaging, or Internet-enabled video chatting seems as nostalgic as the classic rock and disco soundtrack sounds. To be sure, Marrakchi chose this time period in part because it approximated her own adolescence in Casablanca, as she stated in interviews, but also because she knows that the technologies that would soon dominate alter the social environment within which an individual's relationship to the collective takes shape. This is to bring the lessons of Lee and LiPuma's meditation on 'cultures of circulation' back together with the debate that Marrakchi's film produced in Morocco in 2006. Because if Marrakchi's and *Marock*'s 'Moroccanness' were up for discussion, the location of the 'Morocco' in which that debate might take place was no longer immediately clear or perfectly bound. Where is the Internet? Are the boundaries around discussion boards and diasporic conversations clearly marked? To ask these questions at the conclusion of this essay is not in any way to suggest that we have entered a world of open borders and free circulation of ideas, representations and commodities, such as that championed by the steadfast proponents of globalisation and the Internet. It is, rather, precisely because an awareness of questions such as these led some of those who felt deeply uncomfortable by *Marock* to see its arrival in Morocco as inevitable and ineluctable that we must remind ourselves of them. To do so is meant to offer a bulwark against slipping back to familiar modes of reading film and other rich forms of cultural production for 'meaning', as if the social and interpretive worlds they operate in were clearly bound.

Acknowledgements

The research for this paper was funded in part by an AIMS short-term research grant in June–July 2006, for which the author expresses appreciation. Additional support for research travel to Morocco was provided by the Carnegie Corporation of New York. The author thanks Jamal Bahmad, Abdelmjid Kettioui, Sadik Rddad and students in the MA programme in Cultural Studies at Sidi Mohammed Ben Abdellah University, Dhar Mahrez, Fez, for sharing their thoughts on *Marock*. Dilip Gaonkar, Françoise Lionnet and participants at a UCLA Global Fellows seminar read drafts of this essay and offered perceptive comments that helped sharpen its argument; they have his gratitude.

Notes

1. Later in 2006, new legal restrictions against the piracy of Moroccan films made *Marock* harder to obtain in this way. But in 2007, it was still possible to obtain contraband copies of Hollywood and other foreign films openly on Moroccan sidewalks.
2. The director and actor Nabil Lahlou, for example, a harsh critic of the film, stated simply that neither the film nor its director were Moroccan at all (MAP, 2005). Others called for a demand for reimbursement of CCM funds on similar grounds. Nourredine Sail, director of CCM, defended the film and its Moroccanness.
3. In addition to traditional research methods, my research for this essay includes a wide range of web sites, chatrooms, blogs, and Internet reviews. In addition, I opened an online, password-protected discussion of *Marock* with graduate students in cultural studies at Sidi Mohammed Ben Abdellah University, Dhar Mahrez, Fez, where I am an affiliate. I thank participants for sharing a diverse range of views on the film and its controversies.
4. See '"Marock" Sparked Clash in Tangiers' (2005). In Feb. 2006, an Islamist web site, Mejliss al Kalam, further discredited the director by highlighting Marrakchi's apparent support for cartoons representing the Prophet (<http://www.mejliss.com/showthread.php?s=a0c1b0269e7766387faede413d33a917&t=227880>, dated 14 Feb. 2006). 'Magoo 57' (a contributor) rails against Marrakchi for calling herself favourable in the name of freedom of expression ('Leila Marrakchi (sur lle programme de canal + "LA MATINALE*") se dit "*au nom de la liberté d'expression*" à la diffusion des caricature de sidna mohamed (alih salt)'; accessed 10 Feb. 2007).
5. Though she employs a different rubric with respect to understanding Maghribi literature that does not fit within the familiar terms of 'postcolonial' literary studies, the tensions between 'nationalist' and 'nomadic' that animate Valérie Orlando's compelling discussion (2006) of recent francophone Maghribi literature by women seems to me relevant to the present argument.
6. See Edwards (2005a, Chapter 1) for a discussion of Franklin Roosevelt's famous conversation with Sultan Mohammed in terms of racial time and deferral of Moroccan rights; and Chapter 2 for a discussion of the flood of commodities that followed the arrival of American troops in WWII, as well as some Moroccan responses to that flood (such as by Fatima Mernissi, Houcine Slaoui). By promise-threat, I am alluding to Jacques Derrida's formulation in *Monolingualism of the Other*, in which he suggests that a promise is a threat risked.

7. Lee and LiPuma put this efficiently: 'The contemporary decline of the nation-state as the relevant unit of analysis for global capitalism is reflected in two distinct circulatory movements; the increasingly transnational character of labour and the global mobility of finance capital' (2002, p. 208). See also Appadurai (2006).

8. The idea that contemporary Moroccan cultural production not be caught forever in the logic of postcolonialism is not a unique position, but I want to attribute it to Mohammed Dahan, who stated it eloquently at an academic conference at Mohammed V University, Rabat, on 3 Oct. 2004. The setting was a open session following a major conference called 'Urban Generations: Post-colonial Cities' at which Dahan had spoken on 'Cinéma et culture urbaine'. I attended the meeting as well, and draw on my notes. The minutes of the meeting, with Dahan's comment, may be viewed online at: <http://www.open.ac.uk/Arts/ferguson-centre/AfricaNetwork/Documents/mins03october2004tb2.pdf>.

9. See, for example, the collection *Postcolonial Studies and Beyond* (2005).

10. See, for example, the photos at <imdb.com>.

References

Antona, P. (2006) Interview: Laila Marrakchi & Morjana El Alaoui (Marock), <http://www.ecranlarge.com/interview-252.php>.

Appadurai, A. (1996) *Modernity at Large: Cultural Dimensions of Globalisation*, Minneapolis, University of Minnesota Press.

Appadurai, A. (2001) Grassroots Globalisation and the Research Imagination, in A. Appadurai (Ed.) *Globalisation*, Durham, NC, Duke University Press.

Appadurai, A. (2006) *Fear of Small Numbers: An Essay on the Geography of Anger*, Durham, NC, Duke University Press.

Arrighi, G. (1994) *The Long Twentieth Century*, New York, Verso.

Boukhari, K. (2006) Marock: Le film de tous les tabous, *Tel Quel* 223, pp. 40–7.

Cohen, S. and Jaidi, L. (2006) *Morocco: Globalisation and Its Consequences*, New York, Routledge.

Dahan, M. (2006) Letter to Sawt Annass, *Attajdid*, 21–27 May, p. 3.

Derrida, J. (1996) *Le molinguisme de l'autre, ou, La prothèse d'origine*, Paris, Galilée.

Ech-Channa, A. (1996) *Miseria: Témoignages*, Casablanca, Editions Le Fennec.

Edwards, B.T. (2003) Preposterous Encounters: Interrupting American Studies with the (Post)colonial, or *Casablanca* in the American Century, *Comparative Studies of South Asia, Africa and the Middle East* 23(1&2), pp. 70–86.

Edwards, B.T. (2005a) *Morocco Bound: Disorienting America's Maghreb, from Casablanca to the Marrakech Express*, Durham, NC, Duke University Press.

Edwards, B.T. (2005b) Following Casablanca: Recasting the Postcolonial City, *Moving Worlds: A Journal of Transcultural Writings* 5(1), pp. 13–20.

Frank, A.G. (1998) *Re-Orient: Global Economy in the Asian Age*, Berkeley, University of California Press.

Gaonkar, D.P. and Povinelli, E. (2003) Technologies of Public Forms: Circulation, Transfiguration, Recognition, *Public Culture* 15(3), pp. 385–97.

Graiouid, S. (2005) *Social Exile and Virtual H'rig: Computer-Mediated Interaction and Cybercafe Culture in Morocco*, London, Idea Group.

Hansen, M.B. (1999) The Mass Production of the Senses: Classical Cinema as Vernacular Modernism, *Modernism/Modernity* 6(2), pp. 59–77.

Houdaifa, H. and Tounassi, F. (2006) Marock: Le vrai débat, *Le Journal Hebdomadaire* 257, pp. 18–25.

Judy, R.A.T. (1997) On the Politics of Global Language, or Unfungible Local Value, *Boundary 2* 24(2), pp. 101–43.

Khatibi, A. (1971) *La Mémoire tatouée*, Paris, Les Lettres nouvelles.

Larkin, B. (2004) Degraded Images, Distorted Sounds: Nigerian Video and the Infrastructure of Piracy, *Public Culture* 16(2), pp. 289–314.

Laroui, A. (1970) *L'historie du Maghreb: un essai de synthèse,* Paris, F. Maspero.

Lee, B. and LiPuma, E. (2002) Cultures of Circulation: The Imaginations of Modernity, *Public Culture* 14(1), pp. 191–213.

LiPuma, E. and Lee, B. (2004) *Financial Derivatives and the Globalisation of Risk*, Durham, NC, Duke University Press.

Loomba, A. et al. (Eds.) (2005) *Postcolonial Studies and Beyond*, Durham, NC, Duke University Press.

'Marock' Sparked Clash in Tangiers (2005) *Morocco Times*, 19 December, <http://www.moroccotimes.com/> (accessed 29 November 2006).

Mernissi, F. (1998) *Êtes-vous vacciné contre le 'harem'?* Casablanca, Éditions Le Fennec.

Naficy, H. (1993) *The Making of Exile Cultures: Iranian Television in Los Angeles*, Minneapolis, University of Minnesota Press.

Orlando, V. (2006) To Be Singularly Nomadic or a Territorialized National: At the Crossroads of Francophone Women's Writing of the Maghreb, *Meridians: Feminism, Race, Transnationalism* 6(2), pp. 33–53.

Ossman, S. (2002) *Three Faces of Beauty: Casablanca, Paris, Cairo*, Durham, NC, Duke University Press.

Schultheis, B. (2005) Shrek and Miloudi: A 'Glocal' exploration of the Transfiguration Trope. Unpublished conference paper delivered at American Studies Association, Washington, DC, 5 November.

Spivak, G.C. (2003) *Death of a Discipline*, New York, Columbia University Press.

Tanger accueille le huitième Festival du film national: 'Marock' fait scandale (2005). MAP (Maghreb Arabe Presse), 6 December.

Tessler, M. (1993) Alienation of Urban Youth, in I.W. Zartman and W.M. Habeeb (Eds.) *Polity and Society in Contemporary North Africa*, Boulder, Westview.

Zahy, S. (2001) *On ne rentrera pent-être plus jamais chez nous*, Paris, Paris Méditeranée, Casablanca, EDDIF.

Sexual Allegories of National Identity in Nouri Bouzid's *Bezness* (1992)

ROBERT LANG

When Fredric Jameson famously and somewhat controversially observed in his 1986 article, 'Third-World Literature in the Era of Multinational Capitalism', that all third-world texts are necessarily allegorical, particularly when their forms develop out of pre-dominantly western machineries of representation, he argued that they are allegorical in a very specific way—they are to be read as *national allegories*. *'The story of the private individual destiny'*, he wrote, *'is always an allegory of the embattled situation of the public third-world culture and society'* (p. 69, emphasis in original). If we infer from this statement that a third-world culture and society is one that can, very broadly, be defined by its 'embattled situation' (i.e. in relation to hegemonic forces, or a dominant system), we can see, as Jameson himself acknowledged (1987), that '"third-world" cultures' may be found anywhere—in the United States, for example—where the third-world culture in question escapes the categories in which one describes hegemonic culture.[1] The 'larger pre-established identity' within which one might identify differences between two cultural situations (i.e. the differences between a 'first-world' situation and a 'third-world' situation) is identified by Jameson as one in which 'American bankers hold the levers of the world system', a system, 'late capitalism, [that] is the supreme unifying force of contemporary history' (1987, p. 27).[2]

Jameson's article, however, for all its insights, remains problematic for a number of reasons which can only be reconciled with its apparently sweeping generalisations if one is alert to his point that Identity and Difference should not be seen as fixed and eternal opposites (the 'first-' and 'third-world' cultural situations as having nothing in common between them), but rather as inscribed in a dialectical—which is to say mobile—relation to each other. Tunisia both is and is not a 'third-world' country, which puts the country's filmmakers in something of a bind, as they attempt, on the one hand, to speak to a wide range of audiences, and try, on the other, to avoid the intervention of the government censor. Tunisian society is one in which allegory might still be a vitally useful way of participating collectively in a subversive dialogue with one's fellow-citizens, but where in fact audiences yearn to go *beyond* allegory, which, by its very presence in their cinema, attests to the unhappy fact that they are still in an 'embattled situation'.

There is a sense in which we can say that every film ever made is an allegory, because every film presents *a* world, none presents *the* world. And, since there is no reality apart from its representation, every representation is inherently allegorical—or, as Craig Owens observes, turning this fundamental semiotic truth around: 'Allegory ... is revealed as a structural possibility inherent in every work' (1980, p. 64). But one cannot say that all representation is inherently allegorical, and leave it at that, for the term would then lose its usefulness as designating a specific kind of structure. The question, perhaps, is how *self-conscious* an allegory is, and whether that hypothetical creature, the 'average viewer', discerns a film's allegorical aspects as an 'intentional' element among the director's strategies of communication. Of course, a director might not be aware that he or she has made an allegory, or that this or that character, or situation, can be read as 'allegorical', and so one must make the further distinction between political allegory (what, in a loose correspondence, Jameson calls 'national allegory')—allegory that refers to a situation in the public sphere—and ordinary, everyday allegory, a structure that is essentially no different from the psychoanalytic process we call 'identification'.

For an example of the kind of allegorical reading that functions in the private sphere, we might consider why some people love watching prison films. As the author of a popular film studies guide puts it: for such viewers who feel—for whatever reasons—that they have insufficient authority or control over their own lives, the prison film provides a situation with which they can identify and that is in some way analogous to their own situation. How the main character of these films accommodates to the restrictions of prison life—'yet preserves some kind of individual freedom and dignity, by surrender, sly conformity, defiance, or outright intimidation'—provides viewers with a range of options. If nothing else, prison films 'can provide minimal recognition and perhaps compensatory fantasies for people who feel similarly trapped in their own circumstances' (Gollin, 1992, pp. 175–6).

I choose this quite ordinary example of how prison films can function as private-sphere/ personal allegory because I wish to develop a thesis about the allegorical imperative in Tunisian cinema, focusing on Nouri Bouzid's *Bezness*, for there is a dialectic at play in this film (and in many other Tunisian films as well) between themes of incarceration and freedom, inscribed in a discourse on sexuality.[3] Some of the Tunisian cinema's singularity can be found in its willingness—unusual in an Arab society—to present the allegory of the embattled situation of the public third-world culture and society in the private, individual terms of sexuality.

Like the cinemas of most postcolonial societies, that of Tunisia is preoccupied with the politics of emancipation and identity; but in their role as active participants in the construction of a national/cultural identity, the filmmakers find themselves in an increasingly embattled situation on several fronts: the Tunisian public by and large craves an imported, commercial cinema, and the allegorical content of the best Tunisian films is often disdained or ignored. This can be seen not only as a direct consequence of the politics of repression practiced by President Ben 'Ali, but perhaps also as a function of the contradictory status of the image of the body in Tunisia as a Muslim society.

Bouzid has written that he believes 'the body is really the heart of the matter. For the fundamentalists the image of the body is a double prohibition, the prohibition of the image and the prohibition of the body. The body is prohibited, the image is prohibited and the image of the body is double prohibited' (Bouzid, 1996, p. 55). But, he asks: 'Can you make films without the body?' The answer, of course, is: yes—although Tunisian filmmakers are generally not interested in, nor perhaps even capable of, making films without the 'body'. Indeed, in the best Tunisian films the central theme of the filial relationship is expressed through the eroticised or suffering body of the protagonist. Bouzid notes, for example, that in his first film, *Rih al-Sid/Man of Ashes* (1986), the main character Hechmi needs a father, 'but all his fathers cause him problems: his biological father beats him, is violent towards him; his initiation father rapes him; and his spiritual father, Levy, dies' (p. 54). Then, echoing the Tunisian political economist Aziz Krichen in *Le Syndrome Bourguiba* (1992), who himself echoes the Tunisian sociologist Abdelwahab Bouhdiba in *La Sexualité en Islam*, Bouzid observes that: 'With us the problem of the father is associated not with the Oedipus complex but with the myth of Abraham, who was prepared to sacrifice his own son. The son submits to the father and serves him. In our society the individual is nothing; it's the family that counts, the group. Our cinema is trying to destroy the edifice of the family and liberate the individual' (1975, p. 54).

Bezness

The term *bezness* is a generic expression in Tunisia for someone resourceful, or the activities of such a person, who tries to set up a 'small business' with no capital at all. The term is often associated with the activity of hustling, but is not necessarily pejorative. Bouzid's film *Bezness* is an astonishingly daring work that directly confronts the subject of male Tunisians who work as sex hustlers on the streets and beaches of Tunisia's tourist towns, and is additionally interesting for the way in which it invites the viewer to see the film as emblematic and allegorical of Tunisia's precarious economic and cultural position in a rapidly globalising world.

The movie follows the trajectories of three characters in the old city of Sousse—Roufa (Abdel Kechiche), the handsome young hustler; Khomsa (Ghalia Lacroix), his fiancée; and Fred (Jacques Penot), a French photographer. The Frenchman (who is only once referred to by name in the film) wanders about the city, taking photographs, in Orientalist fashion, of its inhabitants. Khomsa becomes his favourite photographic subject, as he finds himself touched by and drawn toward her ambivalence. She is half-attracted and half-repelled by his increasingly relentless pursuit of her, which is both a seduction and, it becomes apparent, also a perversion.

Eventually, the Frenchman is able to lure Khomsa out of the walled city, where she lives, and he drives her to his hotel suite in the *nouvelle ville*. Throughout the film, in snatches of interior monologue, and to her friends, Khomsa expresses her doubts about the Frenchman—what are his real intentions? Will he seduce and abandon her? How similar to, or different from, a Tunisian man is he?—and at the same time, she is fascinated by him and the unnamed possibilities he seems to be offering her. She finds him beautiful, and wonders if she is really tempted by the implication of her friend Ghalia's teasing suggestion: 'Do you like him? It will be more than a sin! He's not even circumcised!'

Meanwhile, Roufa cruises the streets, beaches, hotel swimming pools and nightclubs for female tourists who will pay to sleep with him. In one scene we learn that Roufa knows a police officer whom he hopes will help him get back his passport, which has been seized by the authorities. The officer shows a fatherly concern for Roufa (although, of course, as a police officer—i.e. as a representative of the powerfully repressive state apparatus—he offers Roufa an ambivalent figure of identification). When he gets his passport back, Roufa intends to go to Germany, where, with the help of a former lover, an older German man who lives in Tunisia, he will get a job and save enough money to marry Khomsa. Already, in an irony that is typical of the film, he has bought Khomsa a ring with money he has made from sleeping with European tourists. The officer urges Roufa to stop having sex with men, for the risk of contracting the HIV virus has become too great: 'If you had become a tour guide, and given up [male] prostitution, it would have been better for you ... You only think of one thing, leaving! You'll end up on your knees. A blind man falls ... and then, you want only one thing, to come back!'

The officer, becoming increasingly exasperated, shouts at Roufa: 'Go on dreaming about leaving! [There is] the one who died; the one who is in hiding; the one who is begging; and the one who has caught AIDS. [There is] the one who has become a drug dealer; the one who went to prison; the one who was deported. Only one out of every hundred is saved!'[4] Roufa begs the policeman not to talk about all this: 'I don't want to hear about it! I don't care!' he almost sobs. 'Don't counsel an orphan about how to take care of his soul!' he adds. He reassures the officer that he no longer sleeps with men. Women, he says, are especially attracted to him, making the work relatively easy; moreover, he uses condoms now. When the officer, despite himself, remarks admiringly on Roufa's success as a hustler, Roufa jokes, in a very telling phrase, that 'We are the national wealth! Good for export!' and once more, asks the officer when he might get his passport back.

The hustling scenario, which of course is a reality for many Tunisian young men, is in this film both an emblem of and an allegory for the bigger picture: Tunisia as a third-world country prostituting itself in order to survive in a globalised world in which the economically weak and culturally disadvantaged find themselves nearly overwhelmed—their native or 'traditional' identity compromised or eclipsed—and where (to borrow Jameson's image) 'American bankers hold the levers of the world system'. The tourist industry represents the neocolonial grip of free-market capitalism on Tunisia's destiny, a destiny it shares with all third-world countries in that, precisely, the supreme unifying force of contemporary history is now global. Local governments, when they serve a dictator, are in league with the Father, i.e. are as repressive and castrating, in their own way, as western-led capitalism. Ordinary fathers are powerless to mitigate the destructive impact of economic liberalism on the traditional family (which admittedly is still patriarchal, albeit dysfunctionally so—as Khomsa complains), and young men like Roufa find themselves adrift, without a proper place either in the familial order or in the economic order. Whether or not we wish to ascribe to 'American bankers' (and their clients—corrupt, third-world dictators) the control of 'the levers of the world system', we recognise that in the metaphors of Bouzid's film the paying customer—the tourist—is the one that in the final analysis confers identity. Roufa would not be a hustler, but for the tourists who make his *bezness* possible.

Some of the film's principal themes are organised around the signs of gender and sexuality, as they can be identified in the opening shots. Through the activities of the Frenchman, the Sousse medina is represented as a body to be discovered—penetrated, photographed, investigated. Its labyrinthine streets, its courtyards, its shuttered houses also have their correlative in the city's inhabitants, who are veiled, or silent, or who speak a language he does not understand, or who perform a role (such as 'shopkeeper', or 'hustler') that implies there is another—'true', 'real', 'authentic'—identity underneath or elsewhere, that is inaccessible to the Frenchman because he is a foreigner here. But these natives are not so different, the film says. There are ways in which they are the same as he is; but they are different.

This is why the film contains a motif of the double, which is repeated in the motif of homosexuality. The Frenchman is not only an allusion to Tunisia's French colonial past, which made Tunisia—or a significant portion of its educated, middle classes—a nearly bicultural and bilingual society; he is a representative more generally of the West. Moreover, he can be seen to represent capitalism itself, which is omnivorous and predatory: he photographs men and women, old people, young people, boys and girls, separately and together ... there is almost nothing of this exotic Orient that the Frenchman's hungry camera does not seek to capture, to make a photograph for sale. The Frenchman loves *looking*. His desire is to *see*. He is both a voyeur and a fetishist (as we find out when we see his photograph-filled hotel suite), whose sexuality—if we measure it by a Freudian norm—is no less alienated than that of Roufa, who believes he can sleep with men and women of all ages, *and* love Khomsa, the ultimate prize whom he expects to be a virgin when they marry. Khomsa expresses her doubts that Roufa's subjectivity—his sense of who he is—will not be harmed and confused by this commodification of his body, and by his insistence that personal identity can be located somewhere completely outside the realm of sexual desire.

From Freud, we know that the love of looking—scopophilia—is a component of the sexual drive that exists independently of the erotogenic zones. In the case of the Frenchman in *Bezness*, looking itself as a source of pleasure is clearly represented as an erotic activity, although, in the allegorical reading, what the Frenchman does—his 'taking [of] other people as objects, subjecting them to a curious and controlling gaze' (Mulvey, 2004)—is marked as an Orientalist enterprise, which in the late twentieth century can only refer to the neocolonialism of a western-led globalisation.

The film has a bifurcated point of view. Quite appropriately, the narrator (by which I mean the film itself, or 'Bouzid' as a signifier designating the narrating sensibility) has a foot in both worlds—France/Europe/the West, and Tunisia/the Orient/the third world. The film appears at first to understand the Frenchman, and to understand Roufa and Khomsa as well, giving nearly equal time to the point of view of each, and yet it preserves the final mystery of each—the mystery that each character beholds not only in the other, but in him- or herself. It is perhaps the image of the photograph that expresses best this mystery of identity—the paradox, or conundrum that the *self* can only be discovered and known through the *other*—which the film treats as its central theme.

From Khomsa's point of view, the photograph is an emblem of her alienation, of her 'self' *as* 'other', as described by Roland Barthes in *Camera Lucida*, when he writes that the photograph is 'a cunning dissociation of consciousness from identity' (Barthes, 1981, p. 12): 'No doubt it is metaphorically that I derive my existence from the photographer. But though this dependence is an imaginary one (and from the purest image repertoire), I experience it with the anguish of an uncertain filiation: an image—my image—will be generated: will I be born from an antipathetic individual or from a "good sort"?' (p. 11). Barthes goes on to remark: '[It is] odd that no one has thought of the *disturbance* (to civilisation) which this new action [Photography] causes . . . This disturbance is ultimately one of ownership. Law has expressed it in its way: to whom does the photograph belong?' (pp. 12–13).

Roufa and Khomsa's anxieties—which are essentially the same (for these characters are two expressions of the same side of the 'self'/'other' dialectic that the film explores)—can be summarised as deriving from the relationship of the Tunisian to his or her western 'other', articulated here by Bouzid in a story about the twin mainstays of modern identity: sexuality and the image (or: sexuality in the field of vision). The Frenchman is not unaware of his role in this new development in the evolution of Khomsa's subjectivity, occasioned by the Photograph. When he discovers the meaning of her name (Khomsa—which is related to *khamsa*, the Arabic word for the number five—is the name for 'The Hand of Fatma', a common protective symbol in the Middle East and North Africa, used to ward off the 'evil eye'), he says to himself: 'I have stolen your image. I am a thief!'

The film begins from his point of view. As he plunges into the medina, a labyrinth of narrow streets and dead-ends, a neighbourhood where every door and window he passes is firmly closed—the camera dollying forward, like Alain Resnais' famously probing and insistent camera in *Hiroshima, Mon Amour* (1959), a film to which *Bezness* bears a remarkable resemblance in its preoccupation with cultural and sexual 'difference', and with the question of whether, in the final analysis, it is possible to know the 'other'[5]—the Frenchman reflects, in an interior monologue that we hear in intimate close-up: 'The deeper I go, the more I ask myself questions. And the longer I stay here, the more I feel the journey is complete.[6] Everything is different. The *inside* intrigues me. Everything is veiled. The veil that we wear means nothing . . . it's the *invisible* veil that intrigues me . . . I just can't pierce it. Behind every look is a mystery . . . behind every closed door, a city, a world that eludes me. How do they find their way around?'

In the opening shots of the film, almost the first thing the Frenchman encounters, built into the wall of a house, is a carved relief-sculpture representing the 'evil eye'. To each side of the eye is a fish, and above it, another fish. He pauses for a moment to look at the stone plaque, apparently unaware of, and unconcerned about, its possible meanings. This hieroglyph functions much like the 'No Trespassing' sign that begins Orson Welles's *Citizen Kane* (1941). Not only does the eye have a talismanic function—to ward off evil and protect the inhabitants of the medina from intruders who might bring harm to them—it is a warning to the outsider, the blue-eyed Frenchman, to *beware*. Indeed, in some cultures, where light-coloured eyes are unusual, people with blue eyes are thought to bestow the curse, whether intentionally or unintentionally. The sign on the wall can be seen to refer reflexively to the Frenchman who, (also) with his camera-eye, is marked as a potential threat to the inhabitants of this space.[7]

Following the opening shots of the film, when the Frenchman emerges from the streets of the old city and onto the beach, we see him spying on a young woman wearing a veil (the sign, presumably, that she is local, and Muslim). She stops, puts down her bag, and then suddenly and quite matter-of-factly disrobes, removing her blouse, long skirt, and veil. The woman is wearing a bikini under her clothes, and with an unselfconscious air suggesting that she is a regular visitor to the beach (and which her visible tan-line would seem to confirm), she turns and walks toward the water. From his vantage point, hidden behind a beach kiosk, the Frenchman furtively aims his camera and takes several, quick shots of the woman, who is unaware that she is being photographed. The Frenchman continues his photographing on a more populous section of the beach, where his attention is caught by the image of two female bathers, just a few feet apart, coming out of the water—one, a topless (evidently European) woman, her shoulders pulled back, and striding with a confidence that suggests she is defiantly asserting her right to bare her breasts; and the other, a veiled, Tunisian woman in a dark blouse and ankle-length skirt clinging wetly to her legs, angrily and embarrassedly thrashing her way with difficulty past the European woman, who glances at her, as if in surprise and pity.

In the next couple of shots, Bouzid continues this motif of the European/the Tunisian and his or her double. We see two blond, nearly identical European men in bathing suits. They visually scan the beach, as if looking for something, their heads moving in unison, twin-like. (The framing of this shot suggests that the Frenchman notices them but does not take their photograph—perhaps because he rather resembles them physically, and because he recognises their voyeurism as similar to his own.) The Frenchman aims his camera instead at a blonde, European woman in a deckchair, as she is approached by a group of Tunisian hustlers, who greet her in English. Beyond this scene, we see two good-looking, young Tunisian men coming out of the water. They resemble each other, much as the two blond (I want to say, German) men resemble one another, with whom they present a striking contrast.[8] The Tunisian men, walking toward the camera, are lean, brown and muscular, their genitalia outlined by their bathing suits. The European men (who, perhaps significantly, are seen only from behind) are fair, and slightly soft, their bodies lacking in muscular definition. There is no doubt that Bouzid is creating a sexualised *mise-en-scène* in which the theme of hustling is inscribed in images that acknowledge that sex and commerce, the first and third worlds, and something like fascination with the 'other', are all dialectically linked in Tunisia's tourist industry.

Colonisers and Colonised

The scenes described above lay out the film's core obsessions, much as the Tunisian cultural commentator and film critic Hédi Khélil does with nearly identical preoccupations in his astonishing and scandalous little book, *Sens/Jouissance: Tourisme, Erotisme, Argent dans deux fictions coloniales d'André Gide* (1988). Based on his graduate thesis, 'Des rapports entre colonisateurs et colonisés: Lecture/Ecriture de deux fictions gidiennes, *Si le grain ne meurt* et "Carnets d'Egypte,"' which he defended at the University of Tunis in 1980, Khélil's book confronts the same nexus of tourism, sex, and money that, with similar audacity, Bouzid explores in *Bezness*. Khélil takes up his subject with originality and daring, and with a portion of explicit autobiographical investment that one would never expect to find in a university thesis, least of all one that was successfully defended in a third-world, Arab country.

Khélil, who grew up in Sousse (this beach town where, as we have noted, Bouzid sets his film), begins the description of his project, thus: 'In 1893, André Gide sojourned in two

North African colonies dependent on France. *Tourism* and *pederasty*. Twenty-six years later, he decides to set down on paper his memories of his adventures in Tunisia and Algeria ... Today, a "colonised" reader. His country: Tunisia, former colony of France, *officially independent* and with *a touristic vocation* ... A European author and an Arab reader. Coloniser and colonised. A standard, classic encounter?' (Khélil, 1988, pp. 11–12; emphases in the original). Khélil describes how, when he found Gide's 'Carnets d'Egypte',[9] he devoured everything written by Gide that had in any way to do with North Africa (*Les nourritures terrestres*; *Amyntas*—'Mopsus'—'Feuilles de route'—'Le renoncement au voyage'), but how none of it really grabbed him, because the question that had begun to interest him—*pederasty*, about which he had found scenes in 'Carnets d'Egypte'—was so sublimated as to be for all intents and purposes nonexistent.[10]

Khélil remarks that he was put off Gide's *L'Immoraliste* partly because he was unwilling to identify with Michel, the narrator. In that novel, the line between the narrator and the author is blurred, and it is far from clear whether Michel's position represents Gide's own. That left *Si le grain ne meurt*, an autobiographical work which, alongside 'Carnets d'Egypte', Khélil found to be 'preponderantly' concerned with pederasty. Khélil observes that none of the pioneering works of postcolonial studies confronts the sexual element of the colonial situation: 'Sexual colonisation, no doubt because it takes a more subtle route, has been either simply conjured away by sociologists and historians, or considered as some sort of substitute for economic and political colonisation (which is just another way of making it disappear)' (p. 17).[11] And Khélil notes that while biographies of Gide cannot altogether avoid discussion of his homosexuality, and some, like Dr Jean Delay's *La jeunesse d'André Gide*, even provide a wealth of detail about his relations with adolescent Arabs, they do not address the *colonial* dimension of those relations.

Khélil's book is fascinating precisely because not only does it examine this 'colonial dimension' of Gide's sexual encounters with Arabs in Egypt and North Africa, but because it is written by an Arab who acknowledges his own desire in that Orientalist dialectic which can be found to persist between European and Arab today. Khélil considers the impact of the colonial legacy on his personal and national identity, which he insists is inseparable from questions about his own desire and sexuality, and which is inscribed in a neocolonial relationship that is very apparent in what he calls Tunisia's 'touristic vocation'.[12] And Bouzid's film, as I have suggested, does the same thing. The Frenchman in *Bezness*, and the Tunisian couple Khomsa and Roufa, are, all three, inseparable aspects of the question of the sexual/national identity of the film's viewer/narrator; and the questions Khélil asks about the reader/writer of the Gide text (what he calls *la fiction gidienne*) are in effect the same ones posed by Bouzid in his film. Khélil wonders where one might draw the line between the 'self' and the 'other':

Coming back to tourism and the myth [of an 'Orient' constructed by the West, of which the tourist postcard is the eminent emblem]—what have I tried to do, but seek to identify myself with Gide, to recognise myself in him, make the same journey, follow his itinerary, [and] entreat him sometimes to confer a certain legitimacy on my arguments, at the risk—the serious risk—of occasionally speaking about myself and quite forgetting Gide and his text? How far can one take this specular rapport between 'colonised' and coloniser? Can the 'colonised' know something about his own desires only by deciphering those of the European? To what limit can I push this inquiry into my own reactions as a reader confronting the Gide text?

Wouldn't this [going to/beyond some limit] be committing to a crossing-over that can never be satisfied? Wouldn't this be running the risk of making it a master-game of rules and effects? (1988, p. 128)[13]

Khélil admits that, reading Gide, he finds he is caught up in a play of identifications that makes it impossible for him to recognise himself as either 'European' (as he identifies with Gide the author), or in any sense purely 'Tunisian' (as he identifies with the colonised subject in Gide's text)—these terms, 'European' and 'Tunisian', in any case, being constructions that reveal their radical instability as signifiers as soon as one attempts to define them. He is a hybrid creature:

But the *jouissance* that Gideian pederasty stimulates—is it so complete? Are there not resentments that at times, *après coup*, break my identification with the European's desire? In fact, the perversion of the European's gaze (his voyeurism) and his sexual neurosis (pederasty) never go all the way, never exhaust their pleasure, but oscillate between two attitudes: fascination and repulsion. I feel an intense pleasure in opening myself up to the allure of pederasty. But I tell myself that my own *jouissance*—the *jouissance* of the 'colonised'—is nevertheless triggered by a fiction in which sexual colonisation is at play, a kind of narrative that ought to revolt me, and not give me pleasure. (1988, p. 130)

Khélil adds: 'Now, quite properly, indignation arises at the discovery that I find nothing scandalous in the fact that Mohamed or Mériem serve the sexual requests of the European, since I feel closer to Gide the intellectual than to the colonised. And the pederasty narrative—deep down, I want nothing to thwart it' (1988, pp. 130–1).

But toward the end of his book, Khélil will conclude that Gide, unlike Khélil himself (a colonised subject), will return to—assuming he ever really deviated from—his essentially western character and identity. Khélil reflects that Gide never did understand the problems of the colonised, and remained profoundly a European. His frequent stays in North Africa did not shake that which he held onto most tenaciously, his *'occidentalité'*. Gide's last writings on the Maghrib, Khélil observes, reveal that: 'Ultimately, Africa is nothing in Gide's oeuvre. [But] pederasty is always there. That is the *vérité gidienne*, and not Tunisia, Algeria, or Morocco. Africa is *counterfeit*. No more *speculation* is possible. It is *bankrupt*' (p. 147, emphases in original).[14] But the colonised subject remains forever marked by the colonial encounter. Indeed, he is transformed by it; he is forged within a complex matrix of Oriental/Occidental identifications that will constitute his very identity.

In *Bezness*, we see a similar trajectory made by Bouzid's camera across the lives of the film's principal characters. Perhaps nowhere in the film is the question of personal/national identity made more explicit than in scenes involving mirrors, of which there are several.

The Mirror and Identity

When we first see Roufa, he is bare-chested and still wet from his morning shower. He goes over to a cracked fragment of mirror fixed to the wall of a communal space in the house where he lives with members of his extended family and (we discover later) Khomsa's family, and looks at himself. We will learn that his father is dead, and we see that he appears to have voluntarily filled the position of the head of the household. But there is some ambiguity about how far Roufa's authority extends, or how much it is appreciated, for when he criticises one of his sisters for 'working for other people', his mother tells him not to interfere. It soon becomes clear that his perhaps too heavy-handed exercise of patriarchal authority within the household is resented, for upon seeing him, a male member of his family (a cousin?) will facetiously ask: 'Did his majesty sleep well?' And later, Roufa will get into a nasty argument with his sisters about their general comportment—that one of them smokes cigarettes; and another walks the streets as a prostitute; and that they do not pay enough attention to whether he always has freshly laundered and pressed clothes to wear. His cousin will accuse him on this occasion of 'ruining everything', and tells him to 'stop playing the cock'.[15]

Roufa clearly represents the postcolonial man who, despite his country having gained its independence many years before, knows, and feels most keenly, that he is caught in a neocolonial bind that puts him at a disadvantage. In *Le Maghreb à l'épreuve de la colonisation*, Daniel Rivet, echoing Jacques Berque, describes how the colonised man will often cling to and emphasise certain values, institutions, and discourses that he believes constitute the essence of his identity:

> Colonisation has exacerbated the Maghribi man's masculinity. Deprived of the ability to have his own history, the native compensates by folding himself back into his faith and his sexuality. The woman becomes for him the repository of the values of the conquered nationality. The family offers itself as a refuge where the wounds to his narcissism inflicted by the colonial situation might be tended. If the confining of women is stressed, it is in order to remove them as objects of the conquerors' desire. (Rivet, 2002, p. 303)

Rivet even quotes Berque's remark describing the Maghrib as the 'land of the frustrated impulse', and notes that 'colonisation accentuates the separation of the sexes in town, where contact between the communities is higher' (2002, p. 303). He writes that, according to Eugène Fromentin, for example, 'from the moment the Europeans began to stare at the women dallying on the balconies and roof terraces of Algiers, the men forbade the women to disport themselves there'; and among other examples he offers records that Édouard Michaux-Bellaire noted the same interdiction in Salé (Morocco) during the 1920s, 'to thwart the tourists' voyeurism' (p. 303). Rivet also quotes Sliman al-Jadoui, a *destourien* (a first-generation Tunisian nationalist belonging to the Destour party), who summarised the Tunisian woman's symbolic function in the struggle for Independence, thus: 'Nationality is a secret protected within the women, who remain the bedrock of our social foundation' (p. 304).[16]

Roufa has a proprietary attitude towards Khomsa, and his wish to marry her is bound up with his anxious desire to consolidate an identity for himself as a Tunisian male. The first time the film shows them together is revelatory of Roufa's perhaps unconscious motives. He meets Khomsa on the stairs as he is about to go out, and asks if she will iron his clothes. She warns him that they are not yet married, and she may still change her mind. When he says to her, 'I adore you!' she snaps back: 'Save that for the tourists!' She strongly disapproves of his hustling activities, which he tries to present to her as a legitimate means of making money—money he is earning in order to marry her and put their future life together on a secure financial footing. A little later in the narrative, in a conversation similar to this one, Khomsa indicates that she is fed up: 'This pretence of having "a plan" doesn't cut it anymore. All you do is dream. It's a sham. You're a hustler, and what's more, you're dragging my brother into it!' Khomsa is very fond of Roufa, and may even love him, but one evening when Roufa brings a Dutch woman back to the house, she becomes nearly hysterical with humiliation and rage, and Roufa is forced to take the woman back to her hotel.

The scene reveals much about the real dynamics not only of the bind in which Khomsa and Roufa find themselves, but also—in the allegorical reading—of the bind in which Tunisia itself is caught. As the country tries, from an economically embattled position, to participate in the flows and exchanges of capital that are absolutely vital to its survival in a globalised world, Tunisia quite properly seeks also to maintain its dignity as a society with a culture and national identity befitting a sovereign nation in charge of its own destiny. It is Khomsa's brother Aziz who tips her off that Roufa has brought the Dutch woman back to the house (in a silent and sorrowful gesture, Aziz enters Khomsa's room and closes the window that opens onto the courtyard below, so that his sister will not have to see her fiancé and the woman enter the house together); and after Roufa departs on his motorcycle with the embarrassed woman, we see Aziz, still in Khomsa's room, standing beside the mirror on the wall, his head bowed in shame.

Khomsa angrily tells her brother: 'Go ahead, you, too! Follow him, until you become strangers in your own country!' Her phrasing recalls the title of Julia Kristeva's book, *Strangers to Ourselves* (1991), in which Kristeva reflects on the psychological and social trauma that is often experienced by the foreigner. Kristeva, however, believes that in the late twentieth century, tourism, migrant labour, and modern mass communications have made foreigners of us all—it is no longer possible for an individual, a group, or a nation to remain entirely isolated in a cocoon of particularity—and that this, surely, is a good thing. Clearly, though, if one becomes a foreigner in one's *own* country—in the sense Khomsa means it, of losing even one's primary (national) identity—the task of coming to terms with 'difference' and the 'other' that being a foreigner implies will be more difficult, since the sense of 'self' against which the 'other' is formed is radically unstable. How can Khomsa know if Roufa loves her—loves her above all others—if he performs the act of lovemaking (or sex, 'performed' to resemble lovemaking) every day with European tourists?

Aziz shakes his head in distress, and flees the room, as Khomsa approaches the mirror and looks into it. What follows is a statement of her point of view, offered in an overtly symbolic *mise-en-scène*: the camera pans across her room, taking in a painted frieze on the wall of a caravan of camels and their drivers crossing a desert, and various of her possessions, as we hear her interior monologue on the soundtrack:

> Take me far away ... to where no one will order me about. Let them do whatever they want with me, but not frighten me with their looks. I want to batter the ramparts of the city! And to know its secrets. All my life, I have been reduced to silence. Not a word, not a gesture. In submission to their rule. 'Khomsa, you are a girl. Have you no shame? Khomsa, lower your eyes! Khomsa, get back inside, and close the door! Khomsa, cover yourself! Put up your hair, Khomsa! You have been promised to a man.' A man [the panning camera returns to her reflection in the mirror] ... who confines me within four walls, as women are confined.

When she is finally 'taken away' by the Frenchman, to his hotel in the *nouvelle ville* (or *ville française*, as Khélil tells us it would also be known as by the Tunisians themselves, distinguishing it from the *ville arabe*), we again hear her interior monologue: 'What will he think? You have your universe ... and I have mine. *Everything* separates us.' When, very nervously, she enters his room, and sees all the photographs he has taken of her, she remarks to herself: 'He's mad about taking my picture!' Then, looking at herself in one of the several mirrors in the room, says aloud to herself: 'One day, an important photographer knocked on my door. He wanted to take me to Paris with him. [At this moment, the Frenchman enters the frame.] He departed, and left me behind.' She turns away from the mirror, to face him, and says: 'A foreigner. A transient.'

The Frenchman tries to caress her cheek, but she pulls away from him and turns to face the terrace and look out at the sea. 'The whole world watches me. Not like you, Roufa ... Roufa, the hustler. It's better that I should remain an old maid, than find myself in your bed.' Her voice rises in defiance: 'You will never lock me up! What do they have that is so much better, your tourists? I could beat them all!' The Frenchman gently puts a hand on her shoulder, but her response is ambiguous, reflecting her ambivalence. She reaches, as if to brush his hand away, but instead holds his hand in hers for a moment, as she continues: 'If only there weren't this fear—this fear of people, this fear of myself'.

There will be more scenes in which Khomsa looks at herself in the mirror. But Bouzid creates a symmetry in which Roufa, too, is shown regarding himself in a mirror and responding to his image in a similarly (or rather more extremely) unhappy fashion. (The Frenchman, of course, is never shown looking at himself in a mirror—although it can be said, echoing Jacques Lacan's dictum that 'all sorts of things in the world behave like mirrors' [Lacan, 1988, p. 49], that his photographs function like mirrors.) On the evening that Khomsa does not return home—because she is with the Frenchman at his hotel—Roufa becomes frantic. He searches all over the city for her (a neighbour has told him that she is 'with your photographer friend, the fair-haired boy'[17]). He asks his brother, Navette, 'Where does that fag friend of yours live?' but Navette does not know. Finally, at his wits' end and exhausted, he stops at a bar in the new town and goes to the toilet, where he washes his face in the filthy hand basin. This lavatory, from floor to ceiling, is spectacularly dirty; the tiled walls are streaked with brown marks, and the door is stained with mildew. When he looks at himself in the mirror, which amplifies the hellish wretchedness of the room, he sees an abject figure staring back at him. And when he tries to leave, the doorknob comes off in his hand! He returns to the mirror, looks at his reflection for another, extended moment, and then smashes the mirror with his fist and howls in despair.

The symbolism of such scenes is obvious and needs no comment, although it is worth noting that Roufa's distress is exacerbated by the Frenchman's pursuit of Khomsa, whose recent behaviour strikes at the very core of Roufa's identity as a Tunisian male.

Sexual Allegories of National Identity, and the Dream of Liberation

According to an influential trend in contemporary psychoanalytic theory, the primary way in which it is understood that individual identity is conferred is through the general law of culture that Lacan called the 'Name of the Father'. It is the agency (not to be confused with the 'real' father) that institutes and maintains the law and imposes a sexual identity on the subject.[18] In all dramatic, narrative films—which, because they are representational, and therefore are inherently allegorical—this psychoanalytic law of culture is often figured in stories involving 'real' fathers. In Tunisian cinema of the last 20 years, quite remarkably, we see the question of Tunisian national/cultural identity inscribed in allegories about young men and women with complicated, or troubled, sexual identities, and in stories about 'real' fathers who attempt to maintain the law and impose a sexual identity on their children (or on others over whom they claim authority). As I have suggested, these films, half a dozen of which are notable for being the most daring ever to come out of the Arab world, express some of the difficulties experienced by Tunisia as a post-colonial—and perhaps we should add, Arab—society coping with the western-dominated imperatives of globalisation.

In 1992, five years after President Habib Bourguiba of Tunisia was ousted by his prime minister in a bloodless coup, a curious little book bearing the title *Le Syndrome Bourguiba* was published in Tunis. The book is an indictment of Bourguiba and the 'social system' that the author, Aziz Krichen, believes Tunisia's first president personified. He writes that it is a system marked by 'immaturity' and 'underdevelopment' on nearly every level of national life, including, disastrously and most crucially, the way in which fathers and sons relate to each other. Reproduced on the cover—but nowhere referred to in the book itself—is a picture of a sixth-century stele found in Kasserine, in southern Tunisia, representing the 'Sacrifice of Abraham'. The carved relief-sculpture clearly shows Abraham poised to cut his son Isaac's throat.[19] With his left hand tightly grasping the boy's headscarf, and his right hand holding high above his head a large knife, the rather crazed-looking father is ready to do what he believes his God has asked him to do: sacrifice his son as a burnt offering—to prove his faith, which demands blind obedience to God/the (F)ather.[20]

There are many ways to interpret the story of Abraham and Isaac/Ishmael, and many ways to interpret Krichen's intentions in putting this image on the cover of his book. But two decades years after Bourguiba's ouster, it has to be said that, viewed from a certain angle (such as that of the Amnesty International Reports), Tunisia's politics and government are still marked by the castrating paternalism Krichen describes in his book, and not surprisingly, we find its allegorical correlative in Tunisia's cinema, where problematic filiation is a frequent theme.

Le Syndrome Bourguiba is basically a book of political economy, but it has an unusually psycho-sociological slant, and begins with an analysis of two of Tunisia's best-known films, Bouzid's *Rih al-Sid/Man of Ashes*, and the film he made two years later, *Safâ'h min Dhahab/The Golden Horseshoes* (1988), both of which illustrate or reflect the 'crisis of filiation' that Krichen identifies as both an origin and symptom of Tunisia's continued economic and political 'underdevelopment'. Krichen describes this crisis as the inability to recognise oneself in the father, and the resulting incapacity, in turn, to see oneself in the son (1992, p. 52). He believes not only that Tunisia's colonial experience under the French was infantilising and humiliating for Tunisians, but that it has had a lasting and damaging effect, and that Bourguiba's regime, following Independence, perpetuated the sense of inferiority and dependence that the people had felt under the Protectorate. Krichen's style of writing may at times seem melodramatic, but if we hold to the notion that Tunisian films are allegories of national identity, we can confirm that these films suggest there is a crisis in Tunisian society around questions of national/ cultural identity, brought about, or exacerbated both by the authoritarianism of the (F)ather and the (dialectically related) pressures of globalisation.

In *Bezness*, Roufa's father is dead, but Roufa is not yet himself a father, nor has he been successful in taking his father's place in the family. We have seen how he struggles, on the one hand, to assume the patriarchal responsibilities he believes are expected of him, and how on the other hand he yearns for some kind of personal liberation. We recall Bouzid's observation that 'our cinema is trying to destroy the edifice of the family and liberate the individual' (Bouzid, 1996, p. 54)—and we see that Roufa is caught in a trap that denies him a proper and satisfactory place in society. In one brief, heartbreaking scene, Navette asks Roufa what is troubling him: 'I'm worried about you. Who's getting on your case?' Roufa puts his arms around the boy and says: 'You can't understand'. Navette asks anxiously: 'You don't want me to be around you?' to which Roufa replies, by way of explanation: 'At your age, I used to go to North Beach, in the centre of town. I'd go on foot—that was before all the hotels.' Navette is astonished to learn that there was a time, in the not-so-distant past, when there were no big hotels in Sousse. Roufa continues: 'We were the only people who lived here—us, and Khomsa's family. Our father was alive.' Roufa pauses for a long moment, pondering the meaning of what he has just said. He looks at his young brother, and asks: 'Do you want to be like me?' Navette nods vigorously. With gratitude, and smiling sadly, Roufa hugs the boy tightly, and to hide his emotion, buries his face in the boy's shoulder.

Bouzid invokes the father's memory in this scene in order to link it to the present social and sexual disorder of Roufa's family. Krichen is correct in his analysis that French control during the colonial era was infantilising for Tunisians. But in the neocolonial era, in which countries like France and Germany still control the levers of the world system (as figured in *Bezness* not only by the Frenchman, but also by 'the German'— who, for the very reason that his role is allegorical, is never named—and by the various northern European tourists in the film), an Independent nation like Tunisia discovers that the very meaning of national identity has changed—it no longer means what the nationalists who fought for Independence said or thought it would mean. And certainly, it cannot be defined in an exclusionary manner, as it was, for example, by the Algerians who, starting in the 1930s, adopted the nationalist slogan: 'Islam is my religion, Arabic is my language, Algeria is my fatherland' (cf. Hayes, 2000, p. 1).

When he meets a young European woman in a bar one evening, Roufa tries to hustle her, but she says frankly, and with good humour: 'I like men, but I don't like to be hustled!' She goes on to explain: 'A good-looking guy is part of the trip, part of the fantasy. I'm like you—I like having the choice.' Sensing the truth of her observation, Roufa asks her: 'What do you do in life?' to which she replies: 'I'm in sales'. When Roufa asks her, 'Selling what?' she answers: 'A little of everything, and nothing'. Roufa is silent for a moment. Then, as the camera moves into a close-up of his face, his eyes wide with emotion, he says softly: 'Like me ... I sell a bit of fantasy'. The camera remains fixed on Roufa, as the young woman asks: 'Do you like it?' His voice trembling, he answers: *'I have a family to take care of!'*

This scene, while clearly allegorical, also invites the viewer to reflect on Roufa's sexuality, and adds to our understanding of Khomsa's anxieties regarding his subjectivity, the subjectivity of the hustler. The reflexive fantasy of the 'dream', surely, is one of freedom. (Both Roufa and the young woman, speaking French, use the word *rêve*, although neither of them is a native speaker of the language.) Roufa needs the dream of sexual and subjective freedom as much as the men and women to whom he 'sells' it.[21] Following the scene in which Roufa smashes the mirror in the lavatory at the bar, we see Roufa have a conversation with a musician friend who has just been fired from his job in the orchestra for showing up drunk for work. (The young man suffers from the same malaise as Roufa—the sense of oppression that comes from feeling that one is not in charge of one's own destiny.) Roufa suggests to his friend that he become a hustler, but the young man says it's not for him, adding: 'Each to his own desire'.

When Roufa runs out of ideas, and feels he is losing all hope of extricating himself from his misery (the immediate cause being Khomsa's renewed ambivalence about marrying him; the existential reasons for his unhappiness being unnamed, but turning full circle in the song Navette sings both at the beginning and at the end of the film, about how every hustler eventually grows old), he returns to his former lover, the German. Earlier in the film, we see Roufa introduce a friend of his to the German with the express intention that his friend take his place in the German's affections. But when Roufa arrives at the German's villa and is greeted warily by his friend at the door, Roufa announces that he has changed his mind—he wishes to go to Germany, after all. The friend explains coolly: 'Sorry, everyone has his turn. That's the way it is.'

The conversation that Roufa and the German will have represents the nadir of Roufa's spirit. The German, for his part, is still kind towards Roufa, even though Roufa has on more than one occasion been irresponsible in his dealings with the older man. But as Khélil observes about Gide (as revealed in Gide's last writings on the Maghrib), the German does not—perhaps cannot—understand the problems of the 'colonised'. 'You are mysterious', he says to Roufa, as the young Tunisian tries to explain his distress. 'What are you hiding?' With tears in his eyes, Roufa says that he feels utterly abandoned, and that even his 'dream' has been stolen from him, a dream that no one has tried harder than he to pursue.

The film in the end offers a dispiriting picture of Tunisia's predicament. Khomsa becomes distraught, and seeks to exorcise her demons (is there any other phrase to describe her action of last resort?) by going to a marabout—the tomb of Saint Regaïa—where she joins several other women in need of 'healing', by dancing convulsively to the loud, cacophonous beat of drums and tambourines, until she collapses in a kind of faint. Roufa discovers her there, and at the same time catches sight of the fleeing Frenchman, who had tried to photograph the frenzied spectacle but was forcibly turned away by the woman supervising the therapeutic ritual (or *zar*, as it is known in the Maghrib). In a strange and disturbing scene, Roufa leaves the marabout and follows the Frenchman on his motorcycle. When he catches up with the photographer on the beach, he slowly circles him several times, revving his motorcycle engine in menacing fashion. The two men stare intently at one another—and the Frenchman understands not only that he is under threat, but that he has been the cause of Khomsa's crisis and Roufa's anger. When, having made his point, Roufa eventually drives off, the Frenchman angrily smashes his camera on the side of an upturned boat on the beach and then throws it to the ground. He has gone too far, and knows it. He is the evil eye, after all.

Strangers to Ourselves

There are two scenes in the film that are both funny and painfully revelatory of Tunisia's cultural and economic bind in relation to the West. Early in the film, we see that Roufa has taken it upon himself to teach Khomsa's brother Aziz how to be a hustler. But Aziz reveals himself to be ill-suited for prostitution. He finds that when he tries to hustle a female tourist, he starts to have genuine feelings for her; he cannot properly alienate his sexuality for the task. 'You are really hopeless!' Roufa tells him disgustedly. 'You have to have an eye, and to aim straight!' (Aziz's example suggests, however, that there is hope for Tunisia: in the allegorical reading, not everyone has sold his soul to the devil of western-led capitalist imperatives.) Roufa—who is widely acknowledged by his friends and admirers to be the supreme hustler, the master of his game—decides there and then to show Aziz how it is done. In the scene that follows, however, we see that he may know (or think he knows) the difference between sex for sale and sex as an expression of his authentic identity as a lover; but he no longer necessarily knows who is, and who is not, a Tunisian—which is another way of suggesting that he perhaps no longer knows who he is. The scene, as an allegory, suggests that Tunisian identity has evolved beyond an Orientalist dialectic in which 'self' and 'other' are clearly distinguished.

Roufa singles out a young woman he sees on the Sousse boardwalk, and follows her. She is wearing a short, red skirt and has long, straight hair. She walks with a confident gait, and has a freshness about her that seems to match the sunny weather and the gentle breeze that occasionally blows her hair in front of her eyes. When she stops at an outdoor café, Roufa jumps off his motorcycle and almost runs up to her; and before she can sit down at one of the tables, he takes off his sunglasses and addresses her: 'Hey, beautiful! How do you like the country? Would you like me to show you around?' Affronted, she looks him in the eye for a moment, and turns to leave. He follows her, persisting in his effort to engage her in conversation: 'You know, you really are very beautiful!' he tells her. 'I know a quiet corner not far from here.' She stops, swings around to face him, and says in Tunisian Arabic: 'Who do you take yourself for? Stop being such a jerk!'

Roufa becomes flustered. 'Uh . . . I'm sorry. I never realised you were Tunisian', he stutters. 'It was a mistake, I'm sorry!' And to compound his humiliation, Aziz at that moment catches up with him and says, laughing: 'You're right. You have to have an eye . . . and to aim straight!'

The economic bind in which Tunisia is caught—recalling its infantilising former status as a French protectorate—which is inseparable from the cultural bind illustrated by the scene described above—is expressed with humour in a brief scene toward the end of the film. Navette and one of his young friends compare how the day went for each of them (we have seen Navette doing the rounds of the beach cafés, trying to sell his plush toy camels): 'How much did you make today?' the boy asks. Navette replies: 'I got 5 dinars from my mother and I bought a couple of camels. I sold one to a tourist, an old woman, for a dinar. She asked if I would like to become her son.' Navette's friend is impressed: 'Lucky dog!' he says. 'And so, you accepted?' Quite matter-of-factly, as though the choice were entirely his own, Navette explains: 'No, I don't want to. My brother Roufa would miss me. My mother, too.'

There is no doubt that *Bezness* aims in this 'story of the private individual destiny' to offer 'an allegory of the embattled situation of the public third-world culture and society' of contemporary Tunisia. In the early 1990s—when Tunisia still stood apart from most of the rest of the Arab world as a society that seemed almost unique in the way it deftly straddled the Orient and the West (other Arab countries included Lebanon, and some of the Gulf states, like Dubai), and when culturally and economically it seemed to offer contrasting images of itself as a third-world country that at the same time was not a third-world country—Tunisian cinema was of special interest to the viewer who sees the potential in allegory for resistance to oppression. Tunisia's self-perception, or national narrative, continues to emphasise the country's 'modernity', although by now it is obvious that Ben 'Ali's regime uses this image to distract both the Tunisians themselves and the tourists upon whom the economy so heavily depends from the baleful realities of the police state and the lack of a vibrant public sphere. (Indeed, recognising this, many Tunisians refer to the stagnancy of their public sphere as *le bénalisme*.) As Michel Serceau succinctly observes in his introductory essay, '20 ans déjà!' in the 2004 'Cinémas du Maghreb' issue of *CinémAction*, 'After having been the most progressive of the three Maghrib countries, Tunisia today is the most repressive' (2004, p. 7).

If Roufa and Khomsa, representing a particular postcolonial generation, are in disarray around the question of national identity, there is nevertheless hope for the next generation, represented by Navette, whose nickname refers to a shuttle, something that plies to and fro.[22] There will perhaps be no need, in the future, to choose between (two) identities, to be torn between (two) cultures, to become an exile, like the German in the film, or to feel ambivalent about one's own identity, as Khélil does when he reads André Gide writing about his encounters with adolescent Arabs in Egypt and North Africa. And perhaps, like Julia Kristeva, we shall come to see the liberating logic of being strangers to ourselves.

Acknowledgements

The author thanks Steven Blackburn at the Hartford Seminary and Maha Darawsha at the University of Hartford for their insights into the significance of the story of the 'Sacrifice of Abraham' in Islam. He is grateful to Brian Edwards for his very helpful comments on an earlier draft of this essay, and to David Bond at the Institut des Belles Lettres Arabes (Tunis) for help of various kinds. The origins of this essay go back to 1993 or 1994, when, late one festive evening during the Holy Month of Ramadan, the author met the writer, editor, and publisher Hatem Bourial in the Tunis medina, where he had recently opened a tiny bookshop. Hatem gave him a book he thought he would like, Hédi Khélil's *Sens/Jouissance*, which Hatem had published in his *Passarelles* series. The author acknowledges his gratitude to him for his gift, and for the adventure on which it launched him.

Notes

1. Jameson, in 'A Brief Response', was responding to Aijaz Ahmad (1987). A version of Ahmad's article appeared later as a chapter of his book *In Theory: Classes, Nations, Literatures* (1992). For an example of a third-world society within the United States, consider (large areas of) the city of New Orleans, the discovery of whose third-worldness after Hurricane Katrina in 2005 came as a shock to many Americans. The aftermath of the hurricane—the sluggish and inadequate response of the federal government; and the awarding of major contracts to cronies of the President and others in his political party for the rebuilding of areas devastated by the catastrophe—seemed to confirm the widespread perception that the embattled situation of those most affected by the hurricane and subsequent flooding of the city had been (and continues to be) exacerbated by their third-world status, despite their being citizens of a first-world nation.
2. The original text reads: the first world is based 'far more even than military power, on the fact that American bankers hold the levels [sic] of the world system'.
3. It goes without saying, however, that a prison film made in Hollywood for an American audience is not necessarily going to mean the same thing to contemporary viewers as a prison film made in Tunisia for a Tunisian audience; nor is a film like John Frankenheimer's *The Manchurian Candidate*, made in 1962

(to choose a random example of a boldly allegorical film made in Hollywood), going to signify in the same way as Jonathan Demme's remake of the film in 2004. Frankenheimer's *The Manchurian Candidate* is about the 'strange aftermath of a Korean War veteran's decoration and his mother's machinations to promote her Joseph McCarthy-like husband's career' (Maltin, 2006, p. 830), while Demme's film encourages the viewer to see it as an allegory about big-business string-pulling and the sinister links between the United States government (more specifically, the Bush Administration) and a multinational defence conglomerate that resembles the Halliburton Corporation (cf. Scott, 2004).

4. Throughout this conversation, the male tourists who have sex with hustlers like Roufa are referred to as 'horses'. And later in the movie, when Roufa asks his brother Navette if he knows where Fred lives, Roufa will refer to the Frenchman as 'your horse'.

5. As Bouzid's narrative unfolds, his attention shifts almost exclusively to the point of view of his Tunisian characters, Khomsa and Roufa—which is not necessarily to say that the film abandons the Frenchman's point of view, or that the viewer is expected to see him entirely as the 'other'. Such are the mysteries and vagaries of identification in the film-viewing process that a filmmaker's control over whom or what the viewer identifies with (and when and how) must always remain partial, provisional, contested, and contradictory. Or, to put it another way: while the (skillful) filmmaker exercises considerable control over what the viewer will identify with *formally*, the filmmaker has less control over who and what the viewer will identify with *emotionally*. A film like Clint Eastwood's *Letters from Iwo Jima* (2006), for example, about the World War II Battle of Iwo Jima, from the perspective of the Japanese who fought it, rather proves—on several levels—that, while there are values and emotional structures that might be universal (suggesting that it *is* possible to 'know' the 'other'), each man's 'other', finally, will always be his own. But of course the (im)possibility of 'knowing' the 'other' is an epistemological question—one that might usefully be approached using a complex system of interpretation, such as psychoanalysis—which is to say, it is a universal question, and one that also happens to be at the heart of the Orientalist debate.

6. 'Et plus j'y reste, plus je sens que le voyage est total.' This remark, with the different meanings, or connotations, of '*voyage*', can perhaps be interpreted to mean: 'And the longer I stay here, the more I feel that I am completely out of my element [or far removed from my familiar sphere, country, home, etc.]'.

7. Of course, the plaque is not really intended to serve as protection for the entire medina against the 'evil eye', but rather for the inhabitants of the house only, and perhaps the neighbourhood as well (i.e. any area that falls within its sightlines). Cf. Alan Dundes, 'Wet and Dry, the Evil Eye: An Essay in Indo-European and Semitic Worldview' (1980). It is interesting that in Turkey—which is the former heart of the Ottoman Empire, of which Tunisia was a province—talismans against the evil eye take the form of blue eyes, possibly for the reason that northern Europeans, unaware of local customs, are likely to break the taboo on staring at or praising the beauty of children. (See especially pp. 119–20 of Dundes' essay for this interpretation of the meaning of the blue evil eye, and of the 'like against like' use of blue-eye amulets used in Turkey and surrounding areas.)

8. Since 1990, Germans have comprised the highest number of visitors to Tunisia (an estimated 1 million German tourists visited Tunisia in 1999, for example), although the figures change after the attacks on the World Trade Center in 2001, and the attack on a synagogue in Djerba in southern Tunisia in April 2003, in which 19 people, including 14 German tourists, were killed. A summary of trends following these attacks can be found on ArabDataNet.com (June 2003): 'Travel to Tunisia is dominated by Europeans: of the 5.39 million tourists who visited Tunisia in 2001, more than 3.6 million were from Europe (mainly Germany, Italy, France, and Spain). Of all Tunisia's visitors, Germans are the biggest spenders; German tourists alone provided 38 per cent of total tourism revenues in 2001' <http://www.arabdatanet.com/country/profiles/profile.asp?CtryName=Tunisia&CtryAbrv=tu&NavTitle=Sect or%20Analysis>.

9. 'Carnets d'Egypte' is a travel diary of no more than 20 pages that Gide began on 31 Jan. 1939 and ended during the third week of March of the same year. The diary can be found in the Pléiade edition of Gide's *Œuvres Complètes*. It has never been published in English.

10. On p. 28n10, Khélil notes: 'To avoid all ambiguity, "Pederasty" in this study will always refer to its first meaning ("carnal relations with boys") and never to its broader meaning ("male homosexuality")'.

11. Khélil lists among the pioneering works of postcolonial studies: Albert Memmi's *Portrait du colonisé, précédé de: Portrait du colonisateur*; Frantz Fanon's *Les damnés de la terre* and *Peau noire, masques blancs*; Aimé Césaire's *Discours sur le colonialisme*; and Guy de Boschère's *Autopsie de la colonisation*.

12. '[I am] a "colonised" reader whose own desire is inevitably motivated by the desire of the tourist, in a country where tourism has become a big business, and where, every day, the hotel infrastructure becomes more entrenched and sophisticated, and where a whole repertoire of exotic imagery is sold by travel agencies, brochures, guides, postcards. Any fiction that I might produce—I, who have been "colonised" in my own country—cannot avoid the tourist's gaze, of which one finds several examples in Gide's text' (p. 126).

13. 'La mener ainsi, n'est-ce pas l'engager dans une traversée toujours insatisfaite?' This use of the word *traversée* perhaps intentionally echoes the title of the well-known 1982 Tunisian film, *Traversées/ Crossing Over/Ubûr* by Mahmoud Ben Mahmoud, in which two travellers, a cultivated Arab and an eastern European refugee, find themselves caught in an endless back-and-forth journey on a ferry that runs between Ostend and Dover, because neither the Belgian nor the British authorities will allow them to enter their respective territories. As Kamel Ben Ouanès observes in his 1991 review of the film in *Le Temps* (Tunis), 'It would seem that Mahmoud Ben Mahmoud is saying that our world sees its ideals and its attempts at rapprochement between cultures and between nations come to grief on the rocks of an aborted humanity. The film takes for its premise that there are universal values, and then, from an anthropological perspective, interrogates this premise, examining the nature of human connexion, beyond ethnic and cultural differences, for it is at the frontier, in this no-man's-land *par excellence*, where man finds himself at once outside and in search of a partial-space [*espace-partie*], of an exile-space, or again, of a refuge-space where destiny not only toys with a couple of anonymous figures who have gone astray, but also with the logic of the history of our time, producing antagonisms and collisions between well-provisioned and prosperous nations and others that are underdeveloped and needy' (Touti, 1998, p. 97).

14. These allusions, of course (Africa as *counterfeit*, etc.), are to Gide's novel, *The Counterfeiters [Les faux-monnayeurs]*.

15. The familial identity of this male member of the household is never revealed. He is more or less Roufa's age, but unlike Roufa, who shows anger and frustration at his situation, this young man seems to be suffering from a paralysing psychological depression. Not only is he associated with the caged bird he keeps in the courtyard, he is clearly shown to be an excessive drinker, perhaps even an alcoholic.

16. It is interesting to note that Khomsa never speaks French to the Frenchman (except on one occasion, when she asks him where his wife is), although it is obvious that she understands his language. This is one of the ways in which Bouzid's allegory seeks to present her as an ostensibly 'authentic' representative of a Tunisian culture that has remained untouched and untainted by colonialism. She is the repository of the values of the 'conquered nationality'.

17. The word he uses is '*triglia*', an Italian word that has entered the Tunisian language, referring to a red mullet (*rouget*, in French), which, in this context, is vaguely pejorative, as it is meant to describe the fair-skinned European whose complexion reddens in Tunisia's sunny climate.

18. The best summary of Lacanian psychoanalytic theory as it has been used in film semiotics remains Sandy Flitterman-Lewis' chapter 'Psychoanalysis', in *New Vocabularies in Film Semiotics: Structuralism, Post-Structuralism and Beyond* (pp. 123–83) (from which I have drawn for this definition of the 'Name of the Father').

19. According to Islamic tradition, it is not Isaac, but his brother Ishmael whom Abraham prepares for the sacrifice. (The stele represented on the cover of Krichen's book dates from the sixth century, which is why I refer to Abraham's son here as Isaac.) In any event, the lesson is as much about the necessity of man's submission to the God of his faith as it is about his submission to the authority of the father.

20. The stele includes the 'hand of God' that stops Abraham from going through with the sacrifice; and in the top right-hand corner can be seen the ram caught in a thicket, which God, at the very last moment, provides as a substitute object for sacrifice. As recounted by Marshal Mirkin in a recent article, 'Reinterpreting the Binding of Isaac' (2003), according to the Bible, an angel interceded, saying: 'Lay not thy hand upon the lad, neither do anything to him'. The angel continues, saying: 'For now I know that thou fearest God, seeing thou hast not withheld thy son, thy only son from me'. After the angel speaks, Abraham looks up and sees a ram caught in a thicket.

21. Cf. my chapter, '*Midnight Cowboy*'s Backstory', in *Masculine Interests: Homoerotics in Hollywood Film* (2002, pp. 140–79), in which I examine why Joe Buck, the hero of *Midnight Cowboy* (John Schlesinger, 1969), chooses to become a hustler.

22. The boy's name is Nizq, which does not translate as Navette. Only once in the movie is he referred to as Navette, and it is the Frenchman who calls him this.

References

Ahmad, A. (1987) Jameson's Rhetoric of Otherness and the 'National Allegory', *Social Text* 17, pp. 3–25.

Ahmad, A. (1992) *In Theory: Classes, Nations, Literatures*, London/New York, Verso.

Barthes, R. (1981) *Camera Lucida: Reflections on Photography*, trans. R. Howard, New York, Hill and Wang.

Bouhdiba, A. (1975) *La Sexualité en Islam*, Paris, Quadrige/Presses Universitaires de France.

Bouzid, N. (1996) On Inspiration, in I. Bakari and M.B. Cham (Eds.) *African Experiences of Cinema*, London, British Film Institute.

Delay, J. (1956) *La jeunesse d'André Gide*, Paris, Editions Gallimard.

Dundes, A. (1980) Wet and Dry, the Evil Eye: An Essay in Indo-European and Semitic Worldview, in *Interpreting Folklore*, Bloomington, Indiana University Press.

Flitterman-Lewis, S. (1992) Psychoanalysis, in R. Stam et al. (Eds.) *New Vocabularies in Film Semiotics: Structuralism, Post-Structuralism and Beyond*, London/New York, Routledge.

Gide, A. (1925) *Les Faux-monnayeurs*, Folio 1978, Paris, Editions Gallimard.

Gide, A. (1933–1939) *Oeuvres complètes d'André Gide*, 15, Bibliothèque de la Pléiade, 1997, Paris, Editions Gallimard.

Gollin, R.M. (1992) *A Viewer's Guide to Film: Arts, Artifices, and Issues*, New York, McGraw-Hill.

Hayes, J. (2000) *Queer Nations: Marginal Sexualities in the Maghreb*, Chicago, University of Chicago Press.

Jameson, F. (1986) Third-World Literature in the Era of Multinational Capitalism, *Social Text* 15, pp. 65–88.

Jameson, F. (1987) A Brief Response, *Social Text* 17, pp. 26–7.

Khélil, H. (1988) *Sens/Jouissance: Tourisme, Erotisme, Argent dans deux fictions coloniales d'André Gide*, Tunis, La Nef-Démeter.

Krichen, A. (1992) *Le Syndrome Bourguiba*, Tunis, Cérès Productions.

Kristeva, J. (1991) *Strangers to Ourselves*, trans. L.S. Roudiez, New York, Columbia University Press.

Lacan, J. (1988) *The Seminar of Jacques Lacan, Book II: The Ego in Freud's Theory and in the Technique of Psychoanalysis, 1954–1955*, trans. S. Tomaselli, J.-A. Miller (Ed.) New York/London, Norton.

Lang, R. (2002) *Masculine Interests: Homoerotics in Hollywood Film*, New York, Columbia University Press.

Maltin, L. (2006) *Leonard Maltin's 2007 Movie and Video Guide*, New York, Penguin Books.

Mirkin, M. (2003) Reinterpreting the Binding of Isaac, *Tikkun* 18(5), pp. 61 + [4 pp.].

Mulvey, L. (2004) Visual Pleasure and Narrative Cinema, in L. Braudy and M. Cohen (Eds.) *Film Theory and Criticism*, 6th edn, New York, Oxford University Press.

Owens, C. (1980) The Allegorical Impulse: Toward a Theory of Postmodernism (Part 2), *October* 13, pp. 59–80.

Rivet, D. (2002) *Le Maghreb à l'épreuve de la colonisation*, Paris, Hachette.

Scott, A.O. (2004) Remembrance of Things Planted Deep in the Mind, *The New York Times*, t30 July, <www.nytimes.com/2004/07/30/movies/MANC.html>.

Serceau, M. (2004) 20 ans déjà!, 'Cinémas du Maghreb' issue of *CinémAction* 111, pp. 7–9.

Stam, R. et al. (Eds.) (1992) *New Vocabularies in Film Semiotics: Structuralism, Post-Structuralism and Beyond*, London/New York, Routledge.

Touti, M. (1998) *Films Tunisiens: Longs Métrages, 1967–1998*, Tunis, Répertoire.

The Myth of Masculinity in the Films of Merzak Allouache

ANDREA KHALIL

The construction of the colonial subject in discourse, and the exercise of colonial power through discourse, demands an articulation of forms of difference—racial and sexual. Such an articulation becomes crucial if it is held that the body is always simultaneously (if conflictually) inscribed in both the economy of pleasure and desire and the economy of discourse, domination and power. (Bhabha, 1994, p. 67)

Introduction

In this essay on the mythology of Algerian masculinity I will examine the work of Merzak Allouache who is one of the most well known Algerian filmmakers of the Independence period. Allouache's films focus on many issues of Algerian lives in the post-war period, but most central is the focus on the image of Algerian masculinity and the way masculine desire is informed by discourses of political and religious ideologies. Masculinity is presented through mythic images, produced by ideological discourses, which unravel and become defunct, and which are completely out of sync with the material and historical reality of post-war Algeria. Specifically in *Omar Gatlato* (1976), *Bab el-Oued City* (1994) and *Chouchou* (2002) we see myths of masculinity framed, questioned and denaturalised through an ironic point of view which moves in and out of the frame of the mythic image. The shifting of the image will be understood as the 'image-perception' where perception oscillates between the subjective and the objective (Deleuze, 1986, p. 111). This wavering filmic point of view allows us to see the discrepancy between eternalising myths, or ideologies of male identity on the one hand, and the crushing historical present which prompts new forms of self-representation on the other. The myth of Algerian masculinity is questioned through the visual process of de-familiarisation or denaturalisation of the image.

The denaturalisation of the mythic masculine begins in the first scene of *Omar Gatlato* where Omar states 'I am a man' and then throughout the film, his identification with the mythic Algerian, Arabo-Muslim[1] man is falsified, revealed as artificial, ideological and static. The mythic category 'Algerian male' is visually put into opposition with the *real* subjectivity, an image of fluidity, of dream narrative, of political justice and personal reconciliation, of absolute subjectivity. In *Bab El-Oued* there are two main male characters who allow us to comment on the mythic masculine. Here, two opposing models of masculinity come into conflict, one heavily overladen with ideological definitions, and the other seeking flight, reaching for, and eventually embarking on a sea voyage to Europe. The former, the Islamic male, is represented by Sa'id and the latter, Boualem, struggles in conflict with the Sa'id character and is searching for a new type of manhood, outside of mythical images such as the 'Islamic male'.

The mythification of identity, and Algerian identity in particular, has been examined in works like Malek Alloula's *The Colonial Harem* where the Algerian woman is transformed into an empty form devoid of historical specificity through the colonial photograph. Alloula notes how the French postcard levels the differences between different women, presenting a prototypical Algerian female that conforms to the desire of the French onlooker. In reference to a series of photos (all of the same Algerian woman) Alloula notes how the mythical image is created by a 'saturation' of the French photographer's ideology.

> This slide toward the improbable, caused by the saturation of the image and well beyond the control, is evident in the most flagrant way in a set of three documents in which the same model, wearing the same outfit, photographed by the same photographer at the same location, represents in turn a 'Young Beduin Woman,' a 'Young Woman from the South,' and a 'Young Kabyl Woman ... This incoherent and hasty minglement tells us more than anything else about the photographer's presuppositions and how the postcard functions. (Alloula, 1986, p. 62)

In his text on mythology, Roland Barthes writes about myth as an ideological construction, explaining how myth is a type of semiotic system, a form of communication, not a specific object of representation. In mythological language, ideological representation empties the object of its historical context and transforms it into a natural, necessary and essential form. What happens in the process of mythification of a cinematographic/visual image is that an object which starts as historically and contextually specific can be transformed, through association with an ideological discourse, into an eternal concept that exists outside history, and as a form of Nature as we saw in Alloula's analysis of the Algerian postcards. Take the words (or visual image) representing an 'Algerian woman' or 'Algerian man'. The Algerian man is a contextualised concept, drawing its meaning from identifiable contexts rooted in the history, culture, geography, and language of that definition. While the multiple and historical meanings of 'Algerian man' are productions of identifiable social contexts, through a process of mythification, this very situated meaning is emptied of its specificity when associated with an abstract and unchanging concept: 'Arab Manliness'. This uprooting process transforms the real into the a-historical and Natural state of the so-called 'Arab male', a process which is characteristic of essentialising ideologies (whether nationalist, Orientalist, colonialist, or Islamist) which all share the common goal of fixing identities for their political purposes. Indeed, Allouache's films are framing and responding to myths of manhood created by both Arab Muslim ideology and Orientalist language which the French superimposed on Algeria throughout the colonial period. These films expose both of these mythifying discourses, the impact of the Islamic and nationalist ideologies on the construction of masculinity as well as the impact of colonial language upon the colonial, male subject. Omar in *Omar Gatlato* as well as Boualem in *Bab el-Oued* are two male characters whose story is about not fitting the myth of Algerian male identity and searching for a different form of masculinity.

Although Barthes' analytical vocabulary is quite useful for the analysis of these films, there is a cultural blindness on his part that should be underlined here. Barthes is producing his analysis in the context of the liberal bourgeois society of 1950s France and argues that 'the oppressed', in which definition he rightly associates the proletariat and the colonised, do not have a language capable of mythification. According to his logic, the colonised, or the proletariat, does speak with the depth of language necessary to create a false Nature (a myth). He writes:

> Now the speech of the oppressed can only be poor, monotonous, immediate: his destitution is the very yardstick of his language: he has only one, always the same, that of his actions; metalanguage is a luxury, he cannot yet have access to it. The speech of the oppressed is real ... The oppressed is nothing, he has only one language, that of his emancipation; the oppressor is everything, his language is rich, multiform, supple, with all the possible degrees of dignity at its disposal: he has an exclusive right to meta-language. The oppressed *makes* the world, he has only an active, transitive (political) language; the oppressor conserves it, his language is plenary, intransitive, gestural, theatrical: it is Myth. (Barthes, 1972, pp. 148–9)

This reduction of the colonial languages to an impoverished and utilitarian system, to a thing not able to mythologise itself, reproduces the colonialist negation of the Other, a negation that Barthes is clearly not aligned with, either politically or theoretically. This criticism aside, Barthes' *Mythologies* helps us explain how images of the self are transformed by colonial and Islamic discourses of male identity in post-war Algerian film. These myths are created by Islamic fundamentalist groups, by corrupt governments, by nationalist movements, by various interest groups and clearly by French colonial language about the Algerian people and society. *Omar Gatlato* reads masculinity in Arab culture as a myth, and takes the myth apart, re-historicising the Algerian male as a person caught in a very ideologically treacherous nexus in history.

Some Myths of Masculinity in Algeria

The question of manhood is immediately taken up by Allouache's first film *Omar Gatlato*. In this narrative of 'failed' manhood, we see an implicit or background narrative, that of 'successful' manhood, written under and alongside Omar's story. In this story we see a man stuck in an apartment with a group of women, his mother and sisters, from whom he seeks to escape. When we first meet Omar, the hero of the story, he has not yet become a man according to the convention that defines men in a certain way:

> In the Middle East, sons and daughters grow up in a women's world. Then at the 'age of recognition,' pre-puberty started a scene of expulsion, maturity into manhood marked by an expulsion from women's social space, a process usually starting with expulsion from the women's bath or *hammam*. (Najmabadi, 2006)

Writing this, Afsaneh Najmabadi is inspired by, and quotes, Tunisian sociologist Abdel-wahab Bouhdiba's text on the issues of masculinity, gender relations and sexuality in Islam, *Sexuality in Islam*. In this book Bouhdiba writes that the expulsion of the boy from the world of women, most powerfully enacted by the expulsion from the *hammam*, is a primordial and in fact *the* incipient moment not only defining the entry into manhood but also the borderline to which all of man's subsequent sexual fantasies harken back. Omar is presented in the context of this particular cultural myth of Arab manhood. He lives with these women from whom he is expected to break according to the mythic narrative. Likewise, according to this narrative, Omar is supposed to reach back to that pre-separation period and desire that female flesh from which he succeeded in distancing himself. The heterosexual and mythologising discourse which defines sexuality in the Arab culture *requires him to desire* to return to a physical state of fusion with the female body. Bouhdiba writes: 'What Arabo-Muslim [man] does not remember so much naked [female] flesh and so many ambiguous sensations? Who does not remember the incident by which this world of [female] nakedness suddenly became forbidden?' (Bouhdiba, 1975, p. 168). This expulsion from the world of women *definitively* marks the entry of the (Arabo-Muslim) man into the world of manhood. The 'normal' man's sexuality, or the extent to which a man is masculine, will be measured by the degree to which he fantasises about returning to the lost paradise of women's naked bodies. Bouhdiba writes: 'The most mature man, the most masculine, will never miss an occasion to re-create, to restore, or to rediscover the uterine milieu—whether through memory, mimic, dream or imagination' (p. 168). This narrative is present in *Omar Gatlato*, unconsciously contrasting what Omar does and feels with that normative scenario.

The hypothesis of man's masculinity in the Arabo-Muslim context being founded on the expulsion from the world of women and the continued fantasy of returning to it is taken up in *Omar Gatlato*. This narrative represents the 'mythic man', that which the man is supposed to be in an imaginary and timeless world. However, this mythic male bumps up against Omar's 'real' or historical conditions of existence which is the squalor and poverty of Algiers in the years following the war of Independence. How does the historically situated Algerian male who is forced by his material environment to live in a small apartment with several female members of his family hope to arrive at the mythic definition of manhood which requires that he irrevocably separate himself from the world of the mother?

Omar's first words to us, for he speaks directly to the spectator, are that his name Gatlato means 'macho'. He says he is a 'man', but the rest of the film demonstrates the character's inability to insert himself into that model of identity as it has been defined by various discourses. He cannot perform as a man 'should' perform. Omar's problem, explained verbally and demonstrated visually at the very beginning of the film, is initially presented as a 'failure' to complete the separation from women and the supposed consequence is that he is unable to desire the physical presence of women as objects of desire. The proximity to the world of women is far from being the heteronormative, pre-lapsarian masculine fantasy described by Bouhdiba. As the film progresses, the forced cohabitation of members of the opposite sex is shown to be a result of the social-economic context of over-crowding that was typical of urban Algeria in the years after the war of Independence and result in Omar's problematic experience of his own masculine identity.

The housing crisis of Algiers is referred to in much of the cultural production (raï, film) and ethnography of the 1970s and 1980s. For example, in his book *Men and Popular Music in Algeria*, Marc Schade-Poulsen makes note of the space crisis in Algeria (in the 1980s and 1990s) and the effects that this crisis may have on both sexual and religious norms. His chapter 'Men and the City' is of particular interest here because the author focuses on how two binaries establish men's notions of their masculinity: 'spatial segre-gation of the sexes and the duality of inside and outside . . .' (Schade-Poulsen, 1999, p. 90). Here we see another mythical discourse that is treated as a subtext in *Omar Gatlato*. Schade-Poulsen claims, in the context of his extended ethnographic work in Oran in the 1980s and 1990s, that masculinity in Oran is defined, among other things, by the sexual separation of men and women and by the notion of outside as a masculine (profane) space and inside as a feminine (sacred) space. This mythical (self-) Orientalising definition of gender difference, based on a spatial dichotomy inside/outside, becomes the pivotal form of critique in the film's plot. What happened during the housing crisis in urban Algeria is that the spatial segregation that is supposed to be observed between the sexes begins to break down. Because of the lack of space in the urban areas men and women are forced to cohabitate, thus making for illicit contact between men and women and subsequently forcing a rethinking of the gender-forming narrative. To compensate for this illicit contact, normalcy is restored by the imagined separation between the two sexes.

> In general a man from outside the home seldom entered it directly . . . A member of the family would enter before him to prepare the way . . . In several families with few rooms at their disposal, little notice would be taken of one's presence once one had been introduced because of a common understanding that males and females belonged each to their separate spheres. (Schade-Poulsen, 1999, pp. 90–1)

As an attempt to retain the narrative of gender differentiation for the sake of gender con-struction, the subjects of Schade-Poulsen's ethnography seemed to internally reconstruct the socially regulated sexual segregation, erecting imaginary barriers where there were no physical ones. Omar, in Allouache's film, does not make this normalising adjustment. The male image that conventionally emerges from this male/female, inside/outside, sacred/ profane dichotomous understanding fails to materialise: Omar's inability to become 'a man' comes from the meaninglessness that he finds contained in this discourse of binaries. Behind his *acts* of conventional masculinity, the viewer perceives the emptiness of the dis-course of power and desire. Omar's character shows that the idea of the masculine as pre-viously defined in terms of: separation of the sexes, outside/male and inside/female are mythic and ideological constructions produced by ideologies within Arabo-Islamic culture, and subsequently exploited and reinforced by colonists and Orientalists in their stereotyping drives of domination.

That the film reveals this myth as the false Nature of the Arab male is particularly clear in a scene where Omar gets into an altercation with another man. According to the mythology of the masculine, the outside space is masculine space, a space where man's prowess as a defender of the female private space should be displayed. 'Men occupy a public realm in which honour is protected', while the women are part of a familial 'sacred realm that must be protected' (Ambrust, 2006, p. 205). This mythological construction of manhood is parodied in a scene from *Omar Gatlato*. Omar spends a lot of time outside with his friends, playing music, smoking cigarettes, looking at 'nudie' pictures of girls wearing tight t-shirts and short shorts. In one such scene, a friend of his (one of several male midgets in the film) comes and tells him that there is an unknown man standing around the corner from where Omar and his friends are gathering. Puffing up his chest, Omar goes to kick the guy off the corner and tell him to 'get lost'. However, the scene is silent, with the only sound being the voice-over of the man playing guitar and singing off-screen. The scene mimics the assertion of male prowess, suggesting that Omar is protecting the local girls from this stranger who is waiting outside to prey on them. He mimes his 'male honour' by protecting the female, thus upholding the traditional acts of gender identity. However, we never hear what he is saying to the male stranger. The absence of women and the dialogue which is drowned out by the soundtrack of the friends playing music prompts the viewer to question the seriousness of the action. The scene is de-familiarised by the silence of the characters' words (we just see their lips moving) and the absence of any real women, the two effects creating a scene of total artifice. It is a silent performance: the absence of the women is silently echoed by the absence of sound, the viewer does not hear the men's conversation. It is a myth stripped of its mythological and ideological language. Omar seems to be performing a defunct act of masculine prowess. In addition, the new meaning that this act engenders is that of masculinity as a product of a male–male situation. The physical absence of women does not prevent Omar from playing out his manhood, it rather re-determines the actualisation of his self-identification as a man. The structure of the statement is emptied and the mythical male stands, recognisable and eternal but in front of a total absence of desire to possess a woman. The new content of the male–male relation produces a new meaning in which the male is defined in a homosocial interaction.

Deniz Kandiyoti writes that the effects of sexual segregation upon men can lead to an overzealous desire to come into contact with women. 'A paradox of sexual segregation is that it results in young males' prolonged and promiscuous contact with women and abrupt and possibly disturbing entry into the male world' (Kandiyoti, 1994, p. 204). Although it may be a paradox, the overzealousness is nonetheless a sign inscribed within the norms of 'successful' masculine sexuality in the Arab world. The sexual segregation which characterises Omar's social environment, however, allows for a new desire, a new enactment of masculinity which does not seek contact with women. He increasingly enacts his sexuality with other men while *in the presence of the absent female body*. He does not fantasise about sexual contact with women but rather continually flees it throughout the film. This flight from women is part of a broader suggestion in the film that Omar 'fails' to realise the mythic Arab male identity, a 'failure' which can be read rather as a critical stance *vis-à-vis* the myth. Omar is a reader of myths and shows how his desire has been shaped by the work of Arab and colonial ideologies.

Scenes of homosociality which are both emptied and fulfilling for Omar alternate with scenes of anxiety where Omar comes into physical contact with women. Omar shrinks from any physical contact with members of the opposite sex. This discomfort is seen in the film when Omar is on the bus going to work and a woman, whether accidentally, but more likely on purpose, brushes her hand against his. She is an unveiled woman dressed in western clothes whose hand is holding on to the same bar that Omar is holding. She slides her hand over to Omar's and touches it. Looking shocked and violated Omar jerks his hand away and places it closer to his body, doubling the offended reaction of an elderly, veiled woman who is touched from behind later in the same bus-riding scene. The woman who is ostensibly pinched from behind becomes a mirror image of Omar. Omar's identification with the veiled woman seems to thrust his character into a female subject position, passive, preyed upon and dominated, and at the same time into a desire to retreat into the traditional (mythical) prohibition of contact between the sexes outside marriage. As the pinching gesture occurs off-screen, we only see her reaction. Omar becomes the shadow, the off-screen space of this woman, mimicking her actions and responses. But his desire to withdraw into the prohibition of contact between the sexes is what brings our attention to the sexual-historical moment in which he is living. Young women touch young men on the bus, women divorce their husbands for unknown reasons (as in the case with his sister), men define their manhood, and masculine sexuality, through interactions with other men.

Selma, the Beloved

Omar is first introduced to Selma through the tape recorder that his best friend Moh gives him. In the tape recorder, there is an old tape that Moh forgot to take out and on the tape is the soft voice of a woman who is whispering into the tape recorder. Selma is describing her bedroom, and her feelings at the moment of the recording. Omar hears this while he is unhappily cramped in his tiny bedroom, as if hiding from the world of women and children raging outside this minuscule space. In a moment of triangulated intimacy between a man and a disembodied woman via the male friend, Omar feels a moment of sexual awakening. It is a desire for the female absence that will fulfil his desire for a male presence. The voice turns out to belong to a woman who works with Moh and who gave him the recorder. Selma, we find out, is a secretary and is an active member of the Union. Omar 'falls in love' with her (voice) and convinces Moh to give him her phone number. When he calls her, she answers the phone and he remains silent, not responding right away. Finally he answers her, takes out a comb and begins to comb his hair with it absent-mindedly. Omar has taken her place as the one heard but not seen. He is now the disembodied voice for her to hear, grooming himself during their conversation, suggesting he establishes himself as the absent object of her desiring gaze. While creating that physical absence which seems to be requisite for his desire, Omar assumes the subject position of (female) non-existence. His need for the woman to be physically off-screen allows him to replace his physical body in her place. He enacts here not the desire to possess the female body but rather the dynamic by which his desire for the deficient female body becomes his own sexualised body.

In the next scene, Omar goes drinking with Moh, and he declares he is in love with Selma (whom he still has never seen) and breaks down in tears. Again, Omar is enacting a parody of the myth of heterosexual love while assuming the position of the feminine in this scene. Omar's tears mimic the sorrow of unrequited love from the mythical love between the Arab poet Qais and his beloved Leila. At the same time, his tears transform him into a feminine subject: irrational, chaotic and emotional. To shield Omar from the gaze of onlookers, Moh violently gestures to the waiter to go away, thus protecting Omar from potential male contact. Omar is transformed here into the 'inside', the 'sacred', the conventional 'feminine' that must be protected by the male. This is a moment of femininity in the context of mythical Algerian gender definitions. The designation as feminine as the unreasonable is clearly shown to be arbitrary gender identifications as Omar's actions at once reinforce and defy the accepted mythology that:

> Inside the family, we discover what characterizes its relations to the outside: protection from and regulation of the unreasonable, the latter being associated with femininity rather than with masculinity. A man unable to master these elements in public and private is a man without self-control, a man without control of his femininity. (Schade-Poulsen, 1999, p. 148)

This scene where Omar loses control of his love for Selma is the first narrative moment in the film where masculinity is performed through feminine gender characteristics. Omar is doubly unreasonable because, first, he is crying uncontrollably in public and, second, he is in love with a woman he has never met.

The final sequence of the film, according to narrative convention and expectation, is supposed to be the climax, or *dénouement*. The whole film has been a build-up to this moment where he would meet Selma. He is looking at her from out of sight. In his imagination, a scene unfolds where the two just stand there, Omar looking petrified and Selma staring at him in disgust. The shot is filmed with a coloured lens, emphasising the subjective point of view, Omar's 'coloured' vision of the potential and horrifying meeting. The camera circles around the two characters, in a dizzying, spiralling movement leaving not only Omar, but also the spectator, nauseous and seeking flight from the stifling entrapment of the situation.

The ending does not resolve contradictions by proposing some closure, or a synthesis, but rather dissolves, in a flight from ideological determinations of the self, into an image of pure subjectivity. The imagined scene is one that only Omar, the subject, can see. 'What can be more subjective than a delirium, a dream, a hallucination? But what can be closer to a materiality made up of luminous wave and molecular interactions?' (Deleuze, 1986, pp. 76–7).[2] The dissolution into the pure subjectivity signals a final movement of flight from the ideological, from that molar image described by Deleuze and Guattari in *A Thousand Plateaus* compacted and bound by the defining weight of thought. This character will seek flight into a new, light, molecular mode of being as he runs from the meeting with Selma, running away through the traffic-clogged street. I will return to this dialectical image (molar/molecular) in the discussion of *Bab el-Oued*.

This final scene of *Omar Gatlato* is a visual dissolution of several ideological narratives that Omar has confronted throughout the film. One such idea, the discourse on gender that explains the social and political phenomenon of veiling as an essentially sexual phenomenon, is here put into question. According to this discourse, female beauty and sexuality must be controlled through the veil in order to prevent the eruption of chaos. On this subject Bouhdiba writes: 'Fear of women, anxiety when confronted with the procreative forces that they bear within them, the strange unease that is aroused by that mysterious attraction for an unknown being which is often no more than the unknown of being' (Bouhdiba, 1975, p. 116). This theory is falsified in the final scene of *Omar Gatlato*.

Although he flees the presence of the unveiled Selma, she has neither been presented as a sexualised subject nor as an object of sexual desire. She is a stand-in for what Omar desires *to be*: the Other—female, and if not French, then French-like. She is dressed in modern, western clothing, she is politically and socially active as she works outside the home and is a member of the Union. He needs her *absence* in order to step into her position (as Other) of the sexual subject. The montage in this film continually alternates between Omar and women: the retreat from physical proximity with the woman on the bus cuts to the veiled woman jumping from the pinch, off-screen. Omar becomes the counter-image of the older, veiled woman. Omar desires to become Selma, not the veiled woman, as we see as the film develops. It is not the idea of Selma or her voice that bothers Omar; on the contrary, he desires Selma's *absence*. At the end of the film she is present, and he, from her point of view, is physically absent.

This sexual fantasy is closely tied to the neo-colonialist context in which the film is made. The self–Other relation that we see in Omar's relationship to Selma is reiterant of the colonial ideologies that enmesh the desires to *possess, annihilate* and *become* the colonised Other. The Other is no longer an ontological opposition, no longer an unfamiliar object outside the self. The fissures move from outside into a space of the self which is both interior and exterior, vacillating between the so-called 'self' and the naming 'Other'. The naming, colonising national Other (here conflated with the sexual Other) who spoke of the colonised as sexualised, passive and feminine is here internalised, bringing its discourse (on the Algerian as feminine) *into* the 'becoming' of the self. The 'male' becomes defined in the process of identification through the Other/coloniser/feminine. The becoming of the self is a process realised according to the 'female' identity which was designated to him by the French coloniser. Homi Bhabha's discussion of Franz Fanon can be brought to bear on our understanding of the sexuality of Allouache's male characters:

> It is not the colonialist Self or the colonized Other, but the disturbing distance in-between that constitutes the figure of colonial otherness—the white man's artifice inscribed on the black man's body. It is in relation to this impossible object that the liminal problem of colonial identity and its vicissitudes emerges. Finally, the question of identification is never the affirmation of a pregiven identity, never a *self*-fulfilling prophesy—it is always the production of an image of identity and the transformation of the subject in assuming that image. (Bhabha, 1994, p. 45)

This colonialist transformation-as-becoming of the self through the self/Other and the male/female binaries allows us to see how the postcolonial film comments on the discourses of Orientalism and colonialism. One could understand these films as a form of interiorisation of the Orientalising gesture of Othering. While it is interiorised, it also becomes clearly delineated as a discourse, a historically identifiable discourse that is now part of the self as production. The self is made between French/Arab, male/female, Paris/Algiers. This gesture is carried out with an erotic desire to take in, to physically incorporate the Other: the French, the female. These colonialist binaries rely, according to Edward Sa'id, upon a notion that the opposition of the self and the other is contingent upon the *exteriority* of the Orientalist from the Orient. He writes of the Orientalist: 'What he says and writes, by virtue of the fact that it is said or written, is meant to indicate that the Orientalist is outside the Orient, both as an existential and as a moral fact'

(Sa'id, p. 21). In this film the idea of exteriority and interiority has vanished, leaving a web of connections and cross-identifications within the binaries established by Orientalist thought.

Bab el-Oued and the Death of the Mythic Male

Omar Gatlato is a film made with elegance, subtlety and compassion for its characters who are at once naïve and enlightened about the problems of their society. *Bab el-Oued* is a much more violent film treating its male characters with brutality. It remains an excellent commentary on Algerian myths of masculinity by situating two paradigms of masculinity into conflict, in the form of a confrontation between two characters. One paradigm, represented by the character Sa'id, is the hegemonic, or in the vocabulary of Deleuze, the 'molar' male who serves as a representation of the Islamic myth of masculinity. Sa'id is an Islamic fundamentalist and this is what defines both his gender identity and the hegemonic position he occupies. At the end of the film, Sa'id disappears, signalling perhaps the historic failure of political Islam, but also the death of the myth of masculinity that he propagated.

Sa'id established his position of power in the Algiers neighbourhood of Bab el-Oued by asserting his position as leader of the local Islamic group. Islam, according to this film, produces a masculinity based on violence and oppression of women's (and men's) freedom. 'Hegemonic masculinity is ... a question of how particular groups of men inhabit positions of power and wealth and how they legitimate and reproduce the social relationships that generate their dominance' (Carrigan, quoted in Cornwall and Lindisfarne, 1994, p. 19). The gendered hegemony that structures and represses is a discourse that is here associated with Islam, which is being repressed by a local and global opposition. But within that repressed state, the fundamentalist and his culture of extremist Islam that establishes Sa'id's dominance attempts to dominate with violence. Sa'id rose to power in the neighbourhood of Bab el-Oued after his leadership during the 1988 riots in Algiers. After being apprehended by the police for questioning, it was believed by the inhabitants of Bab el-Oued that Sa'id refused to reveal the names of the riot's organisers despite the pressure put on him by the government. In the years following these riots (historically the period of democratisation and subsequent rise of the FIS), Sa'id became the neighbourhood's Islamic leader and unofficial morality police chief. He stomps through the city checking on the activities of the youth, on the 'Islamic' nature of their activities. He enjoys real authority among the local young men but quickly became seen as an agent of oppression, at one point yelling at one of his followers, Messa'oud (or 'Mess', who is actually a French born Algerian (*beur*) who does not speak Arabic), for looking at a woman passing in the street. He retains tight control over his sister Yamina whom he hits because she spends too much time near the window while hanging out the laundry. He is shown brutalising her and forbidding her from leaving the apartment. Sa'id establishes his power by being the most faithful adherent to a corrupt and intolerant Islam (the only representation posited as possible). Islamic ideology is indicted as the producer of an oppressive, hegemonic mythical masculinity.

In contrast to Sa'id, Boualem is associated with flight from ideological determination, personal justice and the visual element of water in the film. Boualem subverts Sa'id's pseudo-Islamic masculine power by engaging in an illicit affair with Sa'id's sister and by taking down the mosque's loudspeaker which is tied to his roof. In the opening scene of the film, Boualem wakes up in the morning after having worked all night and removes the loudspeaker which projects the voice of the *imam* from his roof. He removes it in an act justified in the narrative by the fact that he works nights and wants to sleep in the morning. From the other building, Yamina, Sa'id's sister and Boualem's love interest, sees him taking the loudspeaker off the roof but does not tell her brother whom she regards as an adversary. Sa'id then organises his followers to hunt down the infidel who committed this act of sacrilege. In the meantime, Boualem and Yamina have a secret rendezvous in the cemetery and Boualem asks Yamina to show him her hair. She takes off her veil and they talk about their future together. Unfortunately for them, one of Sa'id's cohorts sees them and reports the incident to Said. What follows is the face-off between Sa'id and Boualem. Again we are reminded of the mythology of manhood being established through the protection of the woman. But the mythic formula is falsified by virtue of the essential flaw of Sa'id's character. Sa'id's oppressive, hegemonic and corrupt version of masculinity disrupts his legitimacy as protector of women. Our sympathies lie with Boualem who is seeking flight from the sexually, economically and politically frustrating environment created by the fundamentalists.

The relationship between Boualem and Yamina is a red-herring exploration of sexuality. If Boualem were really interested in pursuing a relationship with Yamina he would have avoided the reckless behaviour like meeting in public and asking her to take off her veil. His contact with Yamina seems to be motivated by his desire to come into conflict with Sa'id. Yamina has little importance beyond an instrumental, narrative device for the confrontation between Boualem and Sa'id. Again, the desire, in the form of tension, is between the two male characters, with the woman an absent, third term of the triangle. When Boualem jumps on the boat to flee to Europe at the end of the film, he shows little regret or heartache at leaving Yamina.

What is critical is Sa'id and Boualem's relationship, the two opposing male characters in the film. Sa'id is associated with the binding thoughts of Islamic and corrupt government ideologies: he is the earth, the unjust, the oppressive, defined in *The Image-Movement* as the 'molar' image. Boualem represents water, another state of perception, which is an element of fluidity, light and reconciliation. This film, stylistically aligned with French filmmaking, discovers the freeing image of water, the place to which Boualem flees at the end of the film when he catches the boat to France, capturing the aesthetic of the 'cine-eye':

> Finally, what the French school found in water was the promise or implication of another state of perception: a more than human perception, a perception not tailored to solids, which no longer had the solid as object, as condition, as milieu. A more delicate and vaster perception, a molecular perception, peculiar to a 'cine-eye'. This was the result of starting from a real definition of the two poles of perception: the perception-image was not to be reflected in a formal consciousness, but was to be split into two states, one molecular and one molar, one liquid and one solid, one drawing along and effacing the other. (Deleuze, 1986, p. 80)[3]

The film offers up a new state of perception, a state slit between two states of perception, one liquid, molecular and the other solid, molar, represented by Sa'id, a new view of male sexuality, and man's role in the world. Sexual and political freedom, in the form of dissolution into particles, is sought through flight into the water away from the oppressive atmosphere of Algiers, from the rigid authority of the fundamentalists.

The only real sexual release from the sexual tension between Boualem and Sa'id lies in the homosexual and cross-gender moments. These moments signal the search for an alternative to the paradigmatic Arabo-Muslim gender identity enforced by Sa'id and resisted by Boualem. The women of the block all meet on the rooftops during the day to wash and hang out the laundry. This feminine space turns out to be a homosexual and liminal space when two of the women withdraw into the washing area and one of them starts taking a shower. The other woman, smoking a cigarette while wearing a veil (a favourite image of Allouache's), watches and then helps the other woman wash her body. The female–female erotics of this shower scene is even more explicit in the novel which was written and published in France after the filming took place in Algeria. It is in the same liminal space of the rooftop that a male comedian performs a comedy act for the women. He looks and sounds like a woman which causes the women to erupt in hearty laughter. Same-sex desire and androgyny are the real moments of rebellion against the repression represented and enacted by Sa'id. Even though the homosexual scenes and the cross-gender scenes take little time in the narrative, they touch a nerve that Boualem's character is not able to touch. The hero of an Algerian film cannot (yet) be a cross-dresser. Surely his relationship with Yamina provokes Sa'id's anger, but the homosexual relationships and the cross-gender character provide a profoundly disturbing alternative to the hegemonic heterosexuality that he personifies.

This film was made in Algiers during the Islamic uprising of the early 1990s and in that atmosphere it is not surprising that it condemns Islamic extremism which is conflated, in my view problematically, with Islam itself. In my conversations with Allouache in the spring of 2005, I asked him about this film's representation of Islam. I asked him why there is no representation of a moderate Islam in the film. He replied that he did not know what *un Islam modéré*, or moderate Islam, would mean. Allouache, in this film and others, launches his criticism against Islam through what he shows as the Islamic constructions of masculinity. If *Omar Gatlato* deeply questioned the traditions and discourses of masculinity as defined by Arabo-Muslim tradition, *Bab el-Oued*, although continuous in its rejection of traditional culture's definition of masculinity, more violently and frontally rejects that tradition on the basis of its male identity constructions. In this context of confrontation and total rejection of the Islamic hegemonic male, presented as the only clearly defined paradigm of male identity, there emerges in this film the possibility of cross-gender identity and homosexuality.

This film, more than *Omar Gatlato*, produces and takes sides in a polemical discourse of sexual identity in Algeria. In its wholesale rejection of Islam and Islamic definitions of masculinity the film is allied with an official discourse which throughout the 1990s will increasingly oppose Islamic political representation as well as cultural manifestations. Another red-herring in the film is Allouache's inclusion of the two government-like agents who secretly provide guns to Sa'id. This would make the viewer think that the film is critical of the government's fuelling of the Islamic uprising and its violence against the Algerian population. The film, I would argue, is not anti-government but rather is continuous with a political power that opposes Islamic cultural and political representation within its society. As sinister as these characters appear, their hold on the Islamists is justified by the film.

The position of tacit compliance with the cultural politics of the State by way of an opposition to 'Islamic' definitions of masculinity complicates, by way of a counter-example, the assumption that the intellectual elite is critical of homosexuality. Frédérique Lagrange argues that:

> ... governments and authorities, the media and certainly many writers—necessarily belonging to the 'conscious and educated minority'—feel that their 'educated man's burden' makes it a duty for them to denounce society's defects and corruption (among which homosexuality gets included) and that they should participate, through literature, in the sacred endeavor to reform it. (Lagrange, 2006, p. 191)

That Allouache belongs to this so-called 'conscious and educated minority' goes without saying: Allouache is 'educated', partly in France, and in addition to being a film-maker, he has written the novel version of *Bab El-Oued* (1995) which was published in Paris. He certainly is part of the modern Arab elite that Lagrange is writing about. But, as I have suggested, Allouache is not denouncing homosexuality as a source of corruption and defect. The film shows that the 'social defect' is clearly Islam, which is here reduced to fundamentalist Islam. Although Algerian culture is generally speaking a homophobic culture, any defence of homosexuality couched in terms of a critique of Islam would most likely come from an elite class whose contact with the West and proximity to local power is most pronounced. Ironically then, in the case of Allouache's films, the representation, and to a large degree celebration of homosexuality and cross-dressing, is subversive within the context of an Arabo-Muslim culture which is homophobic, but not in relation to the hegemony that western bourgeois culture enjoys over the Muslim world. His exploration of alternative performances of masculinity and male sexuality is discursively consistent with the political and cultural elite within an Algerian elite allied with the West. Leila Ahmed's argument in *Women and Gender in Islam* will help me illustrate my point with regard to Merzak Allouache. Ahmed explains that in the contemporary Arabo-Islamic world, the popular classes argue for liberation *from the West* through a language of moral purity: adherence to *sunna*, wearing of the veil, rejection of same-sex and extramarital sexuality, and the like. The elite classes (and I situate Allouache in this latter category) argue for liberation *from 'tradition'* using the languages of the western elites. Ahmed writes:

> The pursuit of these goals [of female autonomy] in terms of the language of the Western dress, secularism, and explicit 'feminism' was evidently typical predominantly of the urban middle classes—and consequently 'feminism' as a political movement may perhaps justly be described as 'elitist' or sectional, and cut off from the grass roots of society—whereas women's pursuit of those same goals in the language of Islamism and the veil appears to represent the quest for autonomy at the grass-roots level. (Ahmed, 1992, p. 225)

Analogous to the quest for the feminist movement is the quest for sexual freedom that we see in Alloucahe's films. In this part of her book, Ahmed is describing the debate around feminine identity in the Middle East in the 1980s and 1990s, the same period that is represented in *Bab El-Oued*. The class-based discursive strategies for liberating gender identities are consistent in both cases. In other words, Allouache's film's portrayal of homosexuality as a form of 'liberated' masculinity is not free from its own form of ideological appurtenance. Here he is seeking freedom *from* tradition, not freedom *through* tradition. Positing tradition as the source of oppression and injustice, his point of view is cut off from the grassroots of Algerian and Arab society. It is precisely because Allouache is close both to the cultural and political elite and to western culture that he condemns Islam as *the* defining element of a 'backward' culture and lauds homosexuality in his films. If the centrality of homosexuality as a form of revolt against Islamic culture is not explicit for the viewers of *Bab El-Oued*, it cannot be overlooked while considering his next filmic success, *Chouchou*, to which I will now turn.

J'adooore Chouchou

Allouache's films are progressively more sexual as the masculine character becomes increasingly defined as in movement between the opposing elements: male/female, Arab/French. It is thus not a surprise when at the end of *Chouchou*, the film's main character becomes the happy and fulfilled lover of a high bourgeois Frenchman. This type of self-Orientalising, and self-designation of the self as Other, Bhabha's 'process of identification', of the masculine Arab through the gender and national Other, the French female, both shows the theatrical and performative language of identity and re-enters into the mythological discourse of the Algerian male as sensual, chaotic and willing, desiring to be possessed by the French invader.

For those readers who have never seen *Chouchou*, a box office hit in Paris, this film is a comedy about an Algerian immigrant who arrives in France dressed as a Peruvian, performing and displacing his national Otherness from Algerian to South American. Taken in by some Catholic brothers who live in a monastery, he lands a job as an office assistant to a female psychiatrist who befriends him. Chouchou's character, played by Gad El Mellah, a Moroccan Jewish actor who lives in Paris, eventually confesses to the female psychoanalyst that he wants to live his life as a woman. This comes as no shock to the spectator since Chouchou has basically been dressed as a woman throughout the first part of the film. The psychiatrist encourages him to cross-dress while working in her office and promises him she will heretofore refer to him as *Mademoiselle* Chouchou. Life proceeds as if in a dream for Chouchou, realising his fantasy of 'being' a woman. Chouchou is then spotted by a middle aged, debonair French gentleman, heir to the *grenadine* empire, who falls madly in love with Chouchou. Chouchou in turns falls in love with 'Mr. Grenadine' who soon introduces Chouchou to his parents who absolutely *adoooore* him/her. After some comic interludes and narrative interruptions, the two eventually wed and the film ends in a rather Hollywood-like 'happily ever after' wedding scene. It is a light-hearted comedy, which is quite funny, but with troubling implications about the transformations of an Algerian into the colonial dream of the sexualised, feminised and passive Arab male completely at the disposal of the French bourgeois male. One returns with this film to Bhabha's comment that, with the colonial subject, 'the body is always simultaneously (if conflictually) inscribed in both the economy of pleasure and desire and the economy of discourse, domination and power' (Bhabha, 1994, p. 67).

I would like to focus on two scenes that will demonstrate how the neo-colonialist relation between France and Algeria continues to inform the sexual identification process. This film answers the challenge of manhood posed by homosocial and homophobic societies such as that of Algeria: 'The challenge of manhood is the production of a heteronormative sexuality within the domain of a male homosociality that is always already marked by homoeroticism and is forever under the threat of eroticization' (Najmabadi, 2006, p. 151). This film mocks the Arab heteronormative imperative on sexuality and dramatises the colonial fantasy narrative about the Arab male as sexualised, feminine and ripe for possession by the French conqueror. In this film, French sexual conquest of the passive, feminised Algerian has now become the fantasy of the *Algerian* (Chouchou) who wants to be possessed by the Frenchman. This desire is mediated since the Algerian is played by a Moroccan (who is Jewish) and who dressing up as a Peruvian. Clearly this notion of sexual 'freedom' remains entwined in a discourse of colonial occupation, conquest and servitude.

The first scene that I would like to focus on in this film is a *hammam* scene. The *hammam*, as has already been discussed, is theorised as a critical space of Arab male sexual identity. It is the expulsion from the women's *hammam* that marks the beginning of mythical manhood, and it is the subsequent fantasies about the returning to the uterine world of female nudity that is the measure of the mature man's masculinity. In *Chouchou*, there is a *hammam* scene where the people in the *hammam* are almost-naked transvestites. (The comic effect of this scene comes in part from the observation that it does not take a lot of clothing to make a *transvestite* a transvestite. A small, well placed towel suffices to cross-dress.) The mythical-masculine dream of unity with the female body is here transformed into a dream of unity with male-gendered 'women'. The absence of biological women is filled with the presence of man–women, a fantasy that we first saw in *Omar*. Masculinity is reassured here by the enactment of the *hammam* fantasy, a fantasy altered by the absence of biological women. Once again, it is the absence of the female body that allows the male to actualise his sexuality in a woman's body.

The scene reintroduces the religious element we saw in *Bab el-Oued*. The Arabo-Islamic identity of the characters is clearly and heavily signalled by the language they use. They use Islamic expressions in overabundance: *bismillah, inchallah, la illa il allah*, and the like. They keep repeating these expressions, poking the potential Muslim viewer in the eye. Even though the film is a comedy, I believe that this is part of a broader condemnation of traditional and religious mythifications of masculinity enacted in the film.

The second scene that I would like to point out is when Chouchou, her/his fiancé and the fiancé's parents all first meet at a dinner in a restaurant. Chouchou is very nervous about meeting his future in-laws. What happens at the dinner is astounding and resembles a purely fantasmatic reconciliation between the homo- and heterosexual worlds, but most astoundingly, between the French upper class and the Algerian as under-class. Chouchou misses every high-brow cultural reference made by the *grenadine* parents who are educated in high culture and represent the *haute bourgeoisie française*, or the upper-class French world. Chouchou is a buffoon, but at the same time, charming, cute. He/she is (still) the wild, exotic and uncivilised subject of Orientalism, but tamed and groomed to look good in a fancy French restaurant. By the end of the dinner, Chouchou's jokes and behaviour have put everyone at ease and the in-laws demonstrably 'absolutely adore' their future daughter-in-law. What is disturbing here is that the parents do not seem to notice that Chouchou is Algerian, the ultimate class, race, religious and historical 'Other'. In a kind of wish fulfilment, his Arab identity becomes invisible as the acceptance of his transvestism and homosexuality are accepted by the upper-class educated French parents-in-law. The fantasy enacted in this film is of the socially legitimate bourgeois marriage between a transvestite and the grenadine heir where no one seems to notice his Algerian identity.

It is a dream world of acceptance of Algerian identity masqueraded by his transvestism. His transvestism is satisfying a desire, emerging from the colonial situation, explained Fanon, to be the Other (female), to become the coloniser, to become French, allowing him to play the role of an upper-class French housewife. Transvestism and homosexuality are here instrumentalised as a mode of actualising the desire to fuse with Frenchness. The way in which this film narrativises the desire to fuse with the western Other at the same time posits the Algerian as the enemy, as the strange, even invisible and rejected identity. As an inversion of the Islamic rejection of homosexuality, in *Chouchou* it is the homosexuality that continues to marginalise Algerian/Islamic masculinity.

This film reframes the French, or western, desire about the Algerian man: it is a re-mythification of the Algerian male by the Algerian. The self-Orientalising and repositioning of the Algerian male as object of French, male desire mimic the essentially dark and chaotic 'feminine' created by colonial and Orientalist discourse.

Conclusion

In the remarks above I have noted a narrative progression in three films by Merzak Allouache starting with *Omar Gatlato* (1976) through *Bab el-Oued* (1993) to *Chouchou* (2002). These three films span 26 years, but nonetheless, they form part of a very coherent narrative about Algerian masculinity. I have argued that all three of these films, and in increasing intensity, use male cross-gender identity and homosexuality to falsify a deep-rooted mythology of masculinity created by both colonialist and Islamist ideologies. I have noted, however, that the position being shown through these films is itself enmeshed in ideological discourses. Freedom, both sexual and political, has been associated with the West in these films. This projected equivalence between sexual liberation, gender reconfigurations and western identity reaffirms the colonialist idea that Algerian or Arab culture is despotic, fundamentally lacking in freedom, and barbaric by nature. This discourse is not only similar to the western idea about the despotic East but also to a reaffirmation of the Algerian authority's anti-Islamic and pro-western cultural policies. These films clearly show, progressively, the rejection of Islam and the definitions of gender and sexuality prescribed by tradition (in *Omar Gatlato*), and then a choice of the West over Islamic fundamentalism (Boualem's flight to Europe and his abandonment of Yamina and Sa'id) and a choice of a bourgeois marriage (as a woman) to a French upper-class male for Chouchou.

The periods of colonial occupation, struggles for independence, and the neo-colonial state of affairs have justifiably provoked a rethinking of female gender identities within the Arab world. Western scholars and filmmakers have focused to a large extent on women in the Arab world, making women's oppression, the veil, struggles for equal access to education, and the like the main object of their investigations. However, for whatever reasons, critics and observers have been much less inclined to examine identity transformations in men. I believe that filmmakers like Merzak Allouache are critical since they address the transformations, perhaps equally traumatic and radical, provoked by reconfigurations of masculinity. Because of the patriarchal conventions that have dominated and continue to dominate Arabo-Islamic society, the disruptions to that history by the colonial occupations have caused a fissure in the image of the hegemonic, mythical Arab male that deserves critical scrutiny. In a society that has been historically dominated by masculinist mythology, a look at the reorganisation of the male identity which is treated in these films is crucial for an understanding of contemporary Arab societies.

Acknowledgements

The author would like to express her gratitude to Merzak Allouache for his generous willingness to speak to her on numerous occasions about his films. She would also like to thank Aseel Sawalha, David Kazanjian and Josie Saldana for their readings of this essay.

Notes

1. My use of the term Arabo-Muslim can be defined. The region of the Middle East is both religiously and ethnically diverse. There are Christians, Jews and Muslims. There are Arabs and non-Arabs. There are those who speak Arabic as their mother tongue and those who speak other languages. In this paper I am writing about Arabs and Muslims. However, the word Muslim is used in a culturally descriptive way. I am not presuming the degree of religious adherence or commitment. I am referring to the world view from which this subject position emerged. When I say that a given character is of 'Arabo-Muslim' origin, I am not presuming that the person is religious or practices the religion of Islam. One may be secular in religious orientation but nonetheless from the culture of Arabs and Islam.
2. 'Quoi de plus subjectif qu'un délire, un rêve, une hallucination? Mais quoi de plus proche aussi d'une matérialité faite d'onde lumineuse et d'intéraction moléculaire?' (Deleuze, 1983, p. 111).
3. 'Finalement, ce que l'école française trouvait dans l'eau, c'était la promesse ou l'indication d'un autre état de perception: une perception plus qu'humaine, une perception qui n'était plus taille sur les solides, qui n'avait plus le solide pour objet, pour condition, pour milieu. Une perception plus fine et plus vaste, une perception moléculaire, propre à un "ciné-oeil". Et c'était bien l'aboutissement, dès qu'on partait d'une définition réelle des deux poles de la perception: l'image-perception n'allait pas se réfléchir dans une conscience formelle, mais se scinder en deux états, l'un moléculaire et l'aure molaire, l'un liquide et l'autre solide, l'un entraînant et effaçant l'autre' (Deleuze, 1983, pp. 115–16).

References

Ahmed, L. (1992) *Women and Gender in Islam: Historical Roots of a Modern Debate*, New Haven, Yale University Press.
Allouache, M. (1995) *Bab el-Oued*, Paris, Edition du Seuil.
Alloula, M. (1986) *The Colonial Harem*, Minneapolis, University of Minnesota Press.
Ambrust, W. (2006) Farid Shauqi: Tough Guy, Family Man, Cinema Star, in M. Ghoussoub and E. Sinclair-Webb (Eds.) *Imagined Masculinities: Male Identity and Culture in the Modern Middle East*, London/San Francisco/Beirut, Saqi Books.
Barthes, R. (1957) *Mythologies*, Paris, Editions du Seuil.
Barthes, R. (1972) *Mythologies*, New York, Noonday Press.
Bhabha, H. (1994) *The Location of Culture*, New York/London, Routledge.
Bouhdiba, A. (1975) *La Sexualité en Islam*, Paris, Quadrige/Presses Universitaires de France.
Cornwall, A. and Lindisfarne, N. (Eds.) (1994) *Dislocating Masculinities: Comparative Ethnographies*, London: Routledge Press.
Deleuze, G. (1983) *Cinéma 1: L'image-mouvement*, Paris, Les Editions de minuit.
Deleuze, G. (1986) *Cinema 1: The Movement-Image*, trans. H. Tomlinson and B. Habberjam, Minneapolis, University of Minnesota Press.
Deleuze, G. and Guattari, F. (1987) *A Thousand Plateaus*, Trans. Brian Massumi, Minneapolis: University of Minnesota Press.
Kandiyoti, D. (1994) The Paradoxes of Masculinity: some thoughts on segregated societies, in A. Cornwall and N. Lindisfarne (Eds.) *Dislocating Masculinity: Comparative Ethnographies*, New York/London, Routledge.
Lagrange, F. (2006) Male Homosexuality in Modern Arabic Literature, in M. Ghoussoub and E. Sinclair-Webb (Eds.) *Imagined Masculinities: Male Identity and Culture in the Modern Middle East*, London/San Francisco/Beirut, Saqi Books.
Najmabadi, A. (2006) Reading 'Wiles of Women' Stories, in M. Ghoussoub and E. Sinclair-Webb (Eds.) *Imagined Masculinities: Male Identity and Culture in the Modern Middle East*, London/San Francisco/Beirut, Saqi Books.
Schade-Poulsen, M. (1999) *Men and Popular Music in Algeria: The Social Significance of Raï*, Austin, University of Texas Press.

The Modern Harem in Moknèche's *Le Harem de Mme Osmane* and *Viva Laldjérie*

HAKIM ABDERREZAK

Algerian Women in the Foreground

According to the *Encyclopaedia of Islam*, the word '*harim*' is above all, as its Arabic name indicates, 'a term applied to those parts of the house to which access is forbidden, and hence, more particularly to women's quarters' (1960, p. 209). Whether or not one makes a distinction between the imperial harem and the domestic harem, the imaginary harem and the historical harem, the mythical harem and the political harem, there is one constant that seems to persist: the harem has always been perceived as a space occupied by an ensemble of women dominated by a man. This idea appears in a good number of literary and cinematic representations, whether the works of Maghribis or westerners. But is a harem necessarily the exclusive property of a male master? And if women were to assume control of the harem, what would the consequences be for the society of contemporary Algeria? These are questions that Nadir Moknèche asks in his two full-length films *Le Harem de Mme Osmane* (*Harem of Madame Osmane*) and *Viva Laldjérie* (*Viva Algeria*), which I analyse in this article.

Le Harem de Mme Osmane recounts the story of Madame Bouchama, alias Zhor (Carmen Maura), a former *mudjtahida* (combatant in the War for Algerian Independence), whose old combat name is Osmane. Her husband moved to France, and Zhor is in charge of the house in Algiers. She rents out a few rooms and lives in a section of the dwelling with her adult daughter Sakina (Linda Slimani). She tries hard to manage the property, which houses a group of tenants with conflicting personalities, in an Algeria of social and political turmoil.

Viva Laldjérie uncovers the life of Algerian women at the Debussy Pension in Bab el-Oued, a neighbourhood of Algiers. The film focuses on the fate of three women, Mme Sandjak, alias (la) Papicha (Biyouna), a former cabaret dancer who lives in a nostalgia for *Le Copacabana*, where she used to perform; her daughter Goussem (Lubna Azabal), who shares a room with her mother and tries in vain to convince her married lover Anis to wed her; and Farida Badr, alias Fifi (Nadia Kaci), a prostitute who receives clients in the room next door.

Moknèche is interested in day-to-day life within this feminine universe. His first film, *Le Harem de Mme Osmane*, is set at the beginning of the Algerian Civil War that erupted in 1991, and his second film, *Viva Laldjérie*, takes place near its conclusion in 2003. The political context is intended to reinforce the discomfort of women who were among the most affected by the violence and religious fanaticism that pervaded the country in the 1990s. In both films, women are the victims of massacres and of the overall climate of terror that overcame the country through ten years of intense conflict. The death tool is subject to speculation but estimates range in the tens of thousands. At a time when Algeria was being terrorised by incessant attacks on civilians, when a conservative movement had seized the country, when women were required to become as invisible as possible, Moknèchian women break all kinds of restrictions. Moknèche takes characters that may seem surreal, imbalanced, exaggerated or fantasised, and shows them as constituents of Algerian society. In an interview that accompanies the *Viva* DVD,[1] renowned French historian Benjamin Stora (2004) argues that media representations of Algeria in the last few years have contributed to a monolithic vision of a society that ought to be recognised for its social diversity. He adds that the general absence of films on Algiers during the last 15 years has not helped to rectify these false conceptions. In contrast, Stora observes, Moknèchian cinema foregrounds the Algerian woman in her daily struggle for survival in a society regimented by laws that constrain the social status of women. As Moknèche demonstrates, Algerian society is a society of contradictions, searching for itself amidst the rubble of civil war. The characters are believable, and one needs only look in the streets of Algiers to realise, as does Stora, that Moknèche's filmic vision 'brings us into History'. The reason why it may be difficult to believe that the portraits of women presented to us are the reflections of the Algerian social reality, as the historian emphasises, is because Arab cinema has very rarely directly challenged certain subjects considered taboo. Moknèche, however, does not hesitate to uncover the hidden face of Algeria by putting its marginalised figures on the big screen. *Harem* and *Viva* tackle prostitution, homosexuality, alcohol and liberated sexuality. As Thierry Leclère (2004) writes: '*Viva Laldjérie!* est le premier film de l'histoire du cinéma algérien à montrer des scènes de nu' (*Viva Algeria* is the first film in the history of Algerian cinema to show nude scenes). Indeed, *Viva* is the first Algerian film to show an Algerian woman completely naked, and another engaged in the carnal act with her married lover. In this film, there are many scenes that are unusual in Arab cinema. This approach has elicited several 'virulent interpellations against the director' by Algerians who argue that these are strictly Occidental calamities, utterly foreign to Algerian society. Let us take a closer look and see for ourselves.

Fading Out the Harem

Upon the departure of her husband and son for France, Madame Osmane seeks to perpetuate the institution of the harem. She doubles her efforts so that people will say that 'Mme Osmane knew how to run her harem better than a man'. But the spectator quickly realises that her undertaking is in vain. In the context of terror, state-sanctioned curfews, ingrained traditions, religious fundamentalism and the veil imposed on women, the traditional harem is 'on the verge of collapse', as the cover of the DVD states. The spectator, therefore, is compelled to ask the following questions: what does the end of the traditional harem look like? What is the traditional harem? And what replaces it?

In both *Le Harem de Mme Osmane* and *Viva Laldjérie*, the female characters dream of a new environment and become agents in its formation. The changing environment filmed by Moknèche is a questioning of the classical harem. In effect, the women entice men to enter into 'those parts of the house to which access is forbidden'. From this perspective, the title of the first film is ironic. Nonetheless, it remains a kind of harem, in the sense that in the context of social pressures and threats, the women have to submit themselves to rules of separation of the sexes (such as wearing the veil). But they use these rules to their advantage to transgress secretly within their private space, which allows them to extract themselves from the configuration. Therefore, it is a question of a looser kind of harem, a prototype harem, not a harem *of* women, but a harem *for* women. It is not a question of an imperial or domestic harem, but rather a nascent version of the harem, a novel vision conceived, filmed and brought to the big screen by an Algerian director.[2] The new harem, the atypical harem, the Moknèchian harem, the last generation of harems: all of these are possible appellations for this space revisited by the young director.[3] This harem reflects the changes that have affected the Algerian social fabric these last few years, especially with respect to the roles of men and women. An article published online by *The New York Times* on May 25, 2007 reveals that seventy percent of lawyers in Algeria and sixty percent of judges are women.

I argue that the Moknèchian harem is a 'modern' harem. Before venturing any further, I will explain my choice of the term 'modern'. I use this adjective in the Maghribi sense of the word. In the Arab dialects of the Maghrib, *'moderne'* connotes the idea that the object in question does not fit with, or contradicts, tradition. In addition, in everyday language, 'modern' (used in French) incorporates the notion of a western origin.[4] Hence, the modern harem in Moknèche's cinema is the vision of an Algerian nation in contact with the West. Thus, in these two films, we see a reconfiguration of society that is measured in terms of the redefinition of relationships between men and women and the repartitioning of social space. The traditional harem limits the woman, both physically and symbolically, to the space reserved for her by men. Originally confined to their harem because of their sex, and then for reasons related to their way of life, women are from the outset members of a 'peri-community'. I call these marginalised women 'peri-communitarian' because they have been relegated to the margins for their lifestyle, which does not conform to the socio-religious laws that dominate Algeria. These women are quick to take their destiny in hand and to find their redemption in their marginality, appropriated unto themselves. It is by appropriating their alienated status that 'peri-communitarians' become what I call 'para-communitarians', which is to say that these people embrace their marginality to form a stance against society. As the prefix 'para' implies, they evolve *around* the community, all the while taking an active stand *against* it, in order to better *protect* and conserve their way of life. They are what I call 'marginalists': their fight is a choice of voluntary marginalisation, which translates into a philosophy that threatens to evolve into a self-propagating movement in which the vitality of the marginalised depends not on the drive to reintegrate into the mainstream, but to combat it. Moknèchian cinema displays the valiant struggle of women who, rather than accept their societal destiny, at the heart of society, are determined to assume wholeheartedly their marginality and 'live in sin'. Some take their fight all the way to the grave. A case in point: in *Harem*, Madame Bouchama's daughter, Sakina, goes out after curfew to have fun with her friend Yasmine (Myriam Amarouchène) and as a result she is killed. No matter who is responsible for putting an end to her life, Sakina died for defying the law and refusing limitations symbolised by the roadblock at which she may have refused to stop.

Filming on Location

Both *Harem* and *Viva* represent women in a closed and bounded universe in order to highlight the undesirable status of the peri-community and the chaotic character of the margin. Women are locked up in their buildings, their rooms, keeping their lives far from the community that limits their actions and gestures. The feeling of imprisonment is reinforced by the heat, the large number of tenants, the children who run and move in all directions, the darkness of the hallways and the constriction of the stairwells. Still, the exiguity of the space, intended to recall the deplorable situation of marginalisation, does not present a roadblock for these women. On the contrary, the space of the harem becomes a springboard, a source of strength, and a good reason to flee. In the terms I suggest, they decide to transform their peri-community into a para-community. The long and recurrent water outages that evoke the eternal deficiency of water at the national level and the tightness of the quarters not only recall the lodging shortage in Algeria, but also symbolise the heavy sense of captivity felt by women in particular during the years of ambient conservatism. The fact that Sakina recognises that no one sees anything in the harem where the light lacks intensity, 'one sees nothing here', seems to signify that the characters do not see clearly in the Algeria of the 1990s (the Nation itself is in the dark), and it announces these women's determination to get out of their peri-community (the harem in which they are confined) and to realise a reversal of the situation by getting outside to a space where the thought of a future is possible. The characters' harem is made of neither large rooms, nor open spaces or large gardens: tenants live one atop the other amidst the cries of infants and marital conflicts. Tensions between tenants and close quarters have the effect of reinforcing the sense of promiscuity and enclosure that the idea of the traditional harem suggests. The women feel stifled. They are stifled in the rooms they share with their mothers (as is the case of Goussem and Sakina). They are the flat-mates of people they cannot stand—Mme Osmane tries in vain to get rid of Sid-Ali (Djemel Barek)—and, as for Papicha, she cannot stand having 'a whore' as her neighbour. Finally, they are stifled in their bodies: the wife of the concierge is once again pregnant. It may be appropriate—though crude—to say that she is pregnant to the teeth. Vulgarity seems to be a way of life that the women have assumed to express their disgust with the detention they suffer. They become conscious of the absurdity of their lot in life, which is none other than that of their peripheral status. This consciousness of the suffocating effect of the harem brings about a plan of action. The last drops of water have caused the vase to overflow. These circumstances, which, in fact, affect all Algerians, constitute a detonation for women in particular: for they suffer from it the most. The call to action seems clear. It is time to turn the intolerable classical harem into a modern one. Not only do women physically leave the harem; against the most rigid confinement, they employ the strongest methods. Thus, the women in *Harem* brave the streets, the roadblocks and the fundamentalists. Moknèche's female characters take the liberty to move outside of the harem as they see fit. Night and day, they drive around in a cabriolet, are out in coloured dresses and extravagant gowns. As a result, their confinement has the expression of an overcompensation that is, without a doubt, a tool of para-communitarians to enable their revolt.

Taking the Show on the Road

Even though the country is highly susceptible to ambush and the roads are not safe, the women of *Harem* decide to attend a wedding. They pass through a number of checkpoints, which could very well be false barricades. (A large number of Algerians have lost their lives in massacres by false police officers stationed at fictitious roadside checkpoints.) On the way, they decide to stop in the middle of the countryside. It is precisely this scene that is displayed on the cover of the DVD. The cover, nonetheless, shows the *marabout* (the shrine of a spiritual leader or saint), whereas, in the film it appears only later. The former image depicts the women of the harem posing, in a still shot, dressed in western clothes. Behind the car, one can see the *marabout*. From its position (behind the women), it symbolises the past to which the women literally turn their backs. The *marabout*, on the other hand, is in disrepair, and it appears to disintegrate behind the carefree women. As for their car, it will leave behind in an instant the desolate landscape and the *marabout*, which represents a pious life. Alone and behind the wheel, these women arrive at a colonial-era church in order to celebrate a wedding. Divested of its religious character through its transformation into a hall of festivities by the inhabitants of the region, this church accentuates the modern disposition, hence novelty, of the procession, which celebrates a Muslim wedding in the Christian edifice *par excellence*. The convertible itself is open, freed of its cover; it liberates the women from their confinement before the *marabout*, which remains closed off in the background. The convertible, like an automobile without a veil, opens onto its characters, smiling, determined to follow the road to their individuation. Their poses and their uncovered bodies say much of their desire for freedom, which the cabriolet symbolises perfectly. The camera centres the women, focusing on their bodies, which are literally exposed and highlighted by their colourful, revealing clothes.

Modernity, which is often harshly criticised for its dubious morals, is seen as perverting the woman who exposes her body. This is the discourse of fundamentalists such as the character of Saïd in the Algerian film *Bab el-Oued City* (Allouache, 1994), who sees in the modern 'antenne parabolique' (satellite dish) 'une antenne paradiabolique' (a paradiabolical antenna).[5] In the spoken Arabic of the Maghrib, a woman who allows parts of her skin to be seen is 'naked'. She is quickly admonished, as in *Bab el-Oued City*, to cover herself. In fact, in a scene from Merzak Allouache's film, a mother tells her daughter, while having her try on a dress that she had designed for her, that what would really bring her pleasure would be to see her marry a man from an upscale family. At this very moment, a male teenager perched upon the balcony watches the scene with voyeuristic interest. When his chewing gum pops, the elderly mother discovers and reprimands him, ordering her daughter to cover herself: 'setri rasek' ('protect yourself!'—literally 'protect your head').

When Zhor, in *Harem*, subjected to the perils of the road, exclaims, smothered by the summer heat: 'We can't breathe, we're going to die!' she is alluding to the death that Algerians have met in their cars over the course of the civil war. But she also alludes to the risks inherent in going out 'naked'. Zhor is well aware that in 1993 (the year in which *Harem* is supposed to take place), an unveiled woman goes out at her own risk. The simple fact of leaving the harem is an offence worthy of death.

(Un)Veiling as Action

I would like to call 'portable harem' the veil or the ensemble consisting of the *mansouria* and the *hidjab* (and the *litham* when it is used), to the extent that these are supposed to reconstruct on the outside four walls of the harem, a fortress between the interior and exterior worlds. When she leaves her walls a woman veils herself in order to reconstitute a protective screen around her body which constructs a barrier between her world and the outside in such a way that she will not be seen by men. Thus, she always evolves within her harem, which she carries with her. In contrast, Moknèche's female characters wish to be seen. When they are going to the wedding, they want nothing more than to let down their guard, so to speak, and exhibit their made-up faces, their bodies, their jewellery, and their short western dresses for which they opt over traditional Algerian attire. The women of *Harem* use the portable harem to conceal, not their body, but rather their intention, which is simply to unveil themselves a little later, a little further, a little more.

In Moknèche's films, the headscarf is not worn systematically. That which is designed to cover the totality of the head is more or less placed upon a part of the hair, not to hide it but instead to draw attention. It is worn, so to speak, in the western fashion. One must note that in Maghribi Arabic, that which is modern ('*mod*erne') resonates with that which is 'in style' ('l*mod*a'). It is indeed a matter of style here. Moknèche's films show us Algerian women who are in competition with their Moroccan neighbours over the question of the portable harem. If, in Morocco, feminine magazines such as *Citadine* and television channels like 2M do not hesitate to present Moroccan women with shorter and shorter *jellabas* (called *jabadors*), Algerian women propose to transform the veil into a most original article of fashion. In fact, Meriem tells Mme Osmane that she wants a pink veil. This clearly shows how the Algerian woman has always known how to integrate modernity into her life, even in the most conservative times. Moknèche makes it a point to put this fact in relief by opening and framing *Viva* with images of women in the streets unveiled, lightly veiled, in skirts, etc. The portable harem allows modernity to become part of it and to redefine it. This is particularly obvious in the scene where Goussem uses Fifi's cell phone that the latter carries with her *haïk* (a white traditional veil).

Another purpose of the modern veil is to reveal the para-communitarian woman and her programme of individuation: to define herself as an individual, contrary to the peri-community which veils itself to signify its submission to the law. Its function is reversed and serves the needs of women who have decided to show off their bodies, 'naked', like other women who have come equipped with a readiness to disclose their secrets. The functions of the portable harem for Moknèche are singular. For him, it is a harem for show, whose uses have been modified by his female characters. The women use the portable harem as a camouflage in their quest for individual originality. They put it on and take it off at will, according to the circumstances of their campaigns. Uncertain of what they might encounter on their way to the church, Zhor asks Sakina's friend Yasmine, who was invited to come along to the wedding—'Say, Yasmina, isn't your dress a bit short?—I have a mansouria, just in case. [...]—It's not to vex you. It's in case of a false roadblock'. Yasmine reassures her in her foresight by confiding that if things should go wrong, she had thought to bring her *mansouria*. This long article of clothing, made to be worn outside the house, is for Moknèche's characters, a tool to carry in hand 'just in case', like a shield or a weapon one brandishes in the event of danger. The portable harem makes possible the construction of a para-community, a space against, separated from the ambient state. As Brian Edwards writes, 'the veil is [...] also a symbol of private space, an escape from the national security state [...]' (2005, p. 191). As is the case for every para-community, it is an act of resistance, the tools of a minority in the margins of the meta-community whose regulations, often oppressive, are contested and attacked from the inside. Paradoxically, they veil themselves to escape from the traditional harem and to try to breathe. And it is by using these means put at their disposal by the community (*hidjab, mansouria, litham*) that Moknèche's women attempt to overturn the old harem. The modern harem is a flexible one, adaptable, a harem-chameleon. The para-communitarian harem is similar to an embassy, protected by its foreign status in a country to which it geographically belongs. It is an institution that not only protects them but that can be manipulated by women who confer upon it the form and function they desire. Women-chameleons, they know how to melt into the community, to infiltrate it at will and displace it, along with the concept of the traditional harem.

Like any *para*-communitarian action, it is a gesture of protection, of prime intention: potentially violent, assuredly challenging. Once the roadblocks have been passed, once the destination is reached, the women throw off the portable harem and reveal miniskirts and fashionably tailored dresses, coloured in bright and pastel shades and with impeccable hairstyles that are unsuspected beneath the *mansouria* and the headscarf. The women reproduce the usual sketch of the traditional harem for practical reasons making use of a stratagem to keep the modern harem hidden. Their comportment situates itself between oppositional tactics on the one hand and rebellion and resistance on the other, as defined by Michel de Certeau (1984). Although they try above all to work within the oppressive system, they nevertheless apply their strategy with the definitive goal of changing the principle of the traditional harem itself. The modern harem is, in fact, a harem of circumstance, a harem of appearance, of make-believe. It is a *laissez-passer*, a *carte blanche*, so to speak. Unwilling to reveal their intent, the women make use of the veil to obtain the right to move about freely in the streets. They form a group that passes as a traditional harem (of submissive women) tactically, and that moves beneath the appearance of a harem. It is in fact a mockery of the classical harem, displaying it like some kind of valid documentation to get through checkpoints, in the event of a phoney barricade.

Shooting on the Verge of Modernity

The notion that there is a correlation between modernity, the West, and the emancipation of women is highly controversial, particularly when it is invoked in post-colonial discourse. In pursuing an ethical critique of such discourse, scholars have often elided Maghribi manifestations of this idea. While it is not my intent to promote cultural hegemony, it is nonetheless appropriate to interrogate the cultural implications of Maghribi conceptions of modernity. Feminist Moroccan writer and scholar Fatima Mernissi alludes to this idiom as it is inscribed in the language and the minds of Maghrebis in a passage where she states that the word *hizb* is 'used throughout the Arab world to designate a political party in the modern—that is, *Western* [6]—sense, [and] refers to "any group in which hearts are united and which initiates a common action"'(1993, p. 123). Here, whether it is done in an ironic way or in order to restore the subtle slippage in her text, the author inserts the 'modern-western' equation between two em dashes as if she were mentioning this in passing, whereas her comment is actually central in every sense of the term. Indeed, Mernissi's gesture represents an inference that often goes unnoticed: is it not a systematic conceptualisation 'throughout the Arab world'? The writer later confirms that 'modern' has become synonymous with all that is current, contemporary. Most Algerians and Maghribis use 'modern' to describe the latest (and therefore untraditional) trends of behaviours and habits (such as, for example, women showing skin and smoking) as having been imported from the West.

In Moknèche's films, these links take shape in visual juxtapositions, which illustrate the ways in which modernity does in fact cohabit, or rather imposes and superposes itself in one of the most conservative moments in Algerian history. For example, when the camera sweeps over a company of cars passing through a security brigade, one simultaneously hears blues music and *cha'bi* emanating from two different car stereos. *Cha'bi*, which means 'popular', is traditional Maghribi music, whereas blues in its contemporary form is a modern kind of music that developed in the United States. These two completely different types of music are played as two different feminine types are portrayed: the traditionally veiled woman sits next to a *barbu* in the passenger's seat, whereas the women in western dress are free of masculine chaperones. They do not communicate with each other: each type of woman is in a different car. These women share the cinematic frame, but it is as if they inhabit different places. In a deleted scene from the supplementary material on the second disc of the *Viva* package, Goussem lights a cigarette that is hanging from her lips on the flames from the stove on which coffee is heating in a traditional coffeepot. Free of masculine surveillance, Goussem can indulge in a practice not tolerated of women: she smokes (Sakina is prohibited by her suitor to do so in *Harem*). This visual *bricolage* or *collage* attests to a schizophrenic Algerian duality between tradition and modernity rather than a felicitous cultural diversity that has been able to negotiate both aspects at the heart of the Algerian society. In another portrayal of this duality, Fifi's *haïk* is supposed to *distract from* and *hide* her western dress, high heels and bare skin. Similarly, Fifi wears her *haïk* as a portable harem and hides in the basket she carries a cell phone ('téléphone portable' or simply 'portable' in French), a symbol of autonomy that she holds onto and smuggles into patriarchal society.[7] These filmic *collages* reflect the aspirations of a section of the population that desires to accept, adhere to and identify with a worldview synonymous with novelty in a part of the world where apathy, lack of infrastructure and an absent conception of the future inspire a profound malaise, a general exasperation and a feeling of disgust—'*le dégoûtage*', as they say in the Maghrib, an expression that has come to express a state of mind, a feeling, an outlook on life.

The films of Nadir Moknèche offer original scenarios. His proposed notion of modernity authorises a change in society and the renewal of the institutions it defends. Opposed to modernity—a value enforced by women in Moknèche's work—is the traditional (imposed by men), which is all that the community succeeds in keeping intact.

Of Actors and Extras

In Mernissi's *The Forgotten Queens of Islam* (1993), the sociologist analyses the role of women in positions of power in the Muslim world. Her history concentrates primarily on grand historical figures—often the victims of masculine forgetfulness in the History they write. Though her analysis focuses on prolific monarchs (of States, dynasties, and tribes), her conclusions readily apply to the powerful characters in Moknèche's two films, which portray a hierarchy worthy of the greatest Mernissian palaces. In fact, Zhor does not hesitate to put herself in the role of some great historical figure. She likes to present herself in the skin of high-ranking nobility. For example, when she greets a suitor for her daughter, she talks about herself in the third person: 'Mme Osmane receives everyone. [. . .]', and then says: 'It's not quite the protocol of the Palace of Versailles, but things must be done according to the rules' (which is translated in the film thus: 'This isn't the court of Versailles. But things must be done in the proper manner'). In another sense, Moknèche's harem is a replica of Algerian society. The parallels between the Moknèchian harem and the contemporary nation are striking: the director never forgets to bring to mind the link between the modern harem and the marginalists of the Algerian nation. Mme Osmane's property and the Debussy Pension of *Viva* house different representatives of marginality: they shelter false couples, singles, as well as victims of divorce, adultery and bigamy. These peri-communitarians in Moknèche's films manage to live an original life in spite of everything and thus acquire a para-communitarian status.

We understand the term '*shi'a*' used by the media (more often recognised in the name of 'Shiites') as a sect within Islam. Mernissi remarks that *shi'a* is also the term that applies to a group that centres itself around a leader or 'chief'. This is indeed the case in both films. Yet, as Mernissi states, quoting Ibn Manzur, the author of *Lisan al 'Arab*, the name of 'chief', in its expression here, refers uniquely to a man ('*sha'at al-rajul*'): 'Thus one of the words for wife is *sha'at al-rajul*, she being the *sha'a* of a man because she "follows him and gives him her support"' (1993, p. 123). This expression indicates unambiguously that no woman is allowed to direct a man, a fact that Mernissi contests in her writings, and Moknèche in his cinema. Moknèche's women intend to question this status quo and propose that at the core of the modern harem, it becomes, in fact, otherwise. In each of his films, the harem promotes female governance.

Based on different definitions featured in *Lisan al 'Arab*, Mernissi notes that '*Shi'a* refers to groups that are not in agreement. The *shi'a* are those who see things differently' (1993, p. 123). The non-conformist women in the films express their discord concerning a number of things, but in sum, what they refute is the concept of the traditional gynaecium in which they are forcibly marginalised, and not the modern harem where they seek refuge at will. In order to better appropriate the concept of the harem, they choose to propose a new kind in which the person in power is faced with the impossibility of continuing to perpetuate the traditional one. The women free themselves from the grasp of the man who oppresses, by reforming the roles at the interior of his structure. The women of the Moknèchian harem are therefore in direct contradiction to the very idea of the patri- archal harem. They question the belief that the woman follows the man and force us to envision the flipside of the common expression: *sha'at al-rajul* into *sha'at al-mar'a* (woman as the follower of woman). They prove wrong the idea that women cannot/ may not/should not be heads of power structures in Islamic countries such as the harem and, at a higher level, local, regional and national institutions. The Moknèchian harem puts forth the notion of women who teach themselves and each other the mode of operation of marginalism.

It is because the women are 'disgusted' by the traditional harem that they take the initiative to impose their own freer harem with the fewest possible restrictions and the most possible liberties. It certainly would not be an exaggeration to affirm that the attitude of these women is political. In the very same passage where she shows the contemporary social slippage commonly made between western and modern, Fatima Mernissi makes a very direct connection between *shi'a* and *hizb*: the term *shi'a* itself sometimes appears translated as 'party'. This implies a communal decision to act. The women of the harem have a political agenda. Their behaviour represents a stance taken, and their harem is their political party, one that opposes the traditional harem which is twice represented in *Harem* by the '*barbus*' ('zealots'). The first *barbu* is the man to whom I referred earlier in his car next to his fully veiled wife. The second man finds Meriem wandering through the streets of Algiers at dawn, and he orders her with authority to get lost, to return to that part of society that she is not supposed to leave, to go home. In other words, this man is confronting Meriem, a marginalised singer, to go back into the interior of the community. We must not forget that marginalisation is a means that aims to assimilate the individual more easily once he or she has suffered the entire weight of his or her difference; whereas in the para-community, marginality is perceived as an advantage, as a weapon and an end in itself.

Mistresses, *Femmes* (Quasi-) *Fatales*

With *Harem* and *Viva*, Moknèche proposes to put an end to the idea of man as the un-negotiable master of the harem. He gives women the possibility to occupy this position by entrusting them with the transformation of the traditional harem into a modern one. In the modern harem, it is the woman who directs and controls. A mistress (in the sense of a female master): is such a thing possible? What are the potential ends of such a demeanour? In other words, how does a woman at the head of a harem change the status of women? Does the harem become a para-communitarian harem *for* women (understood either as a place to serve women or a place that shelters them), or *against* women (detrimental to their project)?

The feminine characters regroup themselves around these female chiefs to dethrone men. How is it that the latter are not able to counteract the women's mission? How can a woman take the place of the man in the harem, a place of power and property of the man-master? How can she replace him, and furthermore re-place him somewhere other than at the head of the harem? The proposal of a woman holding the reigns of power is a dangerous enterprise. It is, against all odds, the audacious gamble that Nadir Moknèche makes in his work.

From adolescence, girls are initiated into and instructed in the harem, which is taught indirectly through the mastery of certain arts. For example, Papicha teaches Tiziri the oriental dance of attentive refinement. Thus a 'mistress' in the modern harem is also one who teaches members of her gender how to subjugate men. La Papicha is a schoolmistress, in that she must train a disciple. La Papicha tries to make the modern harem last. To achieve this, she must mould a follower to whom she can pass the torch, choosing the young Tiziri, who admires her: '—Tata Papicha?—Quoi?—Moi, je veux être danseuse ... comme toi.'—(Auntie Papicha?—What?—I want to become a dancer ...

like you.) She conducts the education of the young lady, initiating her in Arab dance and the manners most likely to attract the favour of young men: sensual movements of the hips and protrusion of the bust toward the viewer: 'Tiziri, tu es trop raide, pense à la mer, pense aux vagues! Allez, on reprend! 1, 2, 3, 4, 5 et 6 et 7 et 8, 1, 2, 3, 4, 5 et 6 et 7 et 8 et là tu te penches vers les hommes'. (Tiziri, you're too stiff, think of the sea, think of waves! Come on, let's start over again! 1, 2, 3, 4, 5 and 6 and 7 and 8, 1, 2, 3, 4, 5 and 6 and 7 and 8 and here you bend towards the men.) In one instance, Papicha brings Tiziri with her on an outing in search of *Le Copacabana*. At one point, Papicha asks a young vendor for a *Lion* (a chocolate bar), and he responds that he would gladly offer her a cigarette, but not a *Lion* because a *Lion*, that's too expensive for him. The woman exclaims with an air of astonishment: 'Une cigarette? Un *Lion*, c'est trop cher?' (A cigarette? A *Lion* is too expensive?) and she immediately puts her disciple to the test of subjugating the other sex: 'Tiziri, attaque!' (Tiziri, attack!), after which Tiziri brilliantly executes a few calculated manoeuvres and leaves with her school mistress, and, not with one but two chocolate bars. Tiziri is taught like a lioness to rule over the world of men in order to become the head of the modern kingdom.

Sexuality is not condemned in Islam. It is codified in Algeria (hence restricted to the domain of marriage, even if this is not always the actual case, as the movies clearly illustrate). In hopes of revitalising and regulating the community, society encourages monogamous relationships, but sex for pleasure is strongly discouraged. Moknèchian women question these foundations by not adhering to the rule of fidelity to one man. Instead, assuming the role of the leader of a harem implies forming multiple sexual partnerships consummated in a materialist optic of competitiveness. In a subversive reversal of traditional sexual power relations, Moknèche's vision shows a submissive *man* as a trophy. This trophy is proudly displayed on the mantle of the 'modern' woman. As a matter of fact, Zhor wonders if her authority would have been more respected had she been promiscuous: 'J'aurai dû faire comme Kheïra: mettre des hommes dans mon lit. Mais je n'ai pas voulu'. (I should've done like Kheira: Sleep around. But I wouldn't.) But Zhor's statement is an angry retort to her daughter's analysis of the wider benefits of choosing one's sexual partner(s). In Sakina's view, this ability to choose allows the woman to do such things as live her life, and to pursue sex and love relationship(s) with a man (or men) of her own choosing.

Nonetheless, Moknèche shows the potential danger of attachment. La Papicha is in love with her deceased husband and is vulnerable to the constant criticism of her modern daughter. Goussem despairs over whether she should validate her affection for Anis through the traditional institution of marriage. She constantly urges him to divorce his wife. The film makes it clear that she is wasting her time and her energy: he is married and has at least one other lover. Goussem is following the wrong path, represented by the wrong man, that of a dated harem and a socio-cultural model that is, for all practical purposes, defunct. Beyond its emotional pitfalls, attachment to the wrong sort of man can be physically dangerous. Fifi, having attached herself to 'Chouchou', her 'protector', a national security agent, who wrongly accuses her of stealing his gun, is murdered long before the end of *Viva*. The implication of these two relationships seems to be that a woman should concentrate her efforts on maintaining the para-communitarian harem. Furthermore, should she become involved, the relationship must support this newly formed social framework.

These films give a glimpse of women on the way to mistressing their own destiny. By becoming the female masters and mistresses of men, by transforming the classical harem into a harem for women, they allow themselves the possibility to actualise their individuation.

Same Cast, Different Scenario

In order for the traditional harem to give way to the modern harem, there must be a role reversal and a rearrangement of power assignments. The women take the dominant role at the head of the harem. Committed to not reproducing the exclusive power structure of the traditional harem, the women share authority in the utter exclusion of men. The para-communitarian harem is an institution in which the structure is inverted and the hierarchy is negotiable. Often those who hold the reigns of power (Mme Osmane) or are expected to (Papicha) have to let go of the ropes to their daughters or other women so that they may do as they see fit. They are likely to complain of tensions that result, which are expected to arise given the framework of a formation that must simultaneously *direct* to stay on course, and *confer* a large number of liberties onto its members.

The modern harem is effectively a place of expression for women. Meriem, the domestic worker, threatens her mistress: 'Je serai jamais ta Fatma!' (I'll never be your Fatma!). This kind of behaviour is tolerated because the rebellion is not directed against Zhor, but instead against the traditional harem that is synonymous with the oppressive structure of the colonial regime, which Meriem's use of the generic colonial term 'Fatma' implies. Meriem warns that she will not fill the traditional role of domestic servant in the atypical structure of the modern harem. Hence, Meriem goes to answer the door, and in a fit of anger, turns on her heel decidedly, leaving Nasser, Sakina's lover, at the door, unannounced.

Every respectable colonial harem, Malek Alloula tells us, must have an Odalisque:

> The word *odalisque*, which begins to appear in French at the beginning of the seventeenth [*sic*] century, comes from the Turkish *odaliq* [*sic*], meaning chambermaid (from *oda* = chamber). Initially a chambermaid or a slave in the service of the women of the harem, the odalisque was metamorphosed by Orientalist painting (see Jean Auguste Dominique Ingres) into the sublimated image of the one enclosed by the harem. This jewel of the prohibited space is endowed by the Western imagination with a strong erotic connotation (1986, note 24, p. 130).

In the modern or post-colonial harem, another inversion is operating: the Odalisque reclaims her status as a freed woman. Meriem is the complete opposite of that which an odalisque or Fatma represents in the colonialist signification. She is not a 'chambermaid' in the typical sense: she is always seen outside of the rooms, out in the car, on the sidewalk in front of the house, in the courtyard. She even leaves the house without prior permission of Madame Bouchama, who asks her where she is going, to which she answers nonchalantly that she is going to fetch an ice cream. From the opening scene, Meriem defiantly marks her role as a *dışarlık kadın* (literally an odalisque of the exterior).[8] Indeed, she sings in a corner of the courtyard avoiding her chores that await her inside the villa. The doors of the harem do not enclose her; furthermore, Meriem is never far from opening them. Concerning the 'strong erotic connotation' described by Alloula, this image evaporates in front of a *dışarlık* such as Meriem who is dirtily dressed, is no longer youthful, displays unrefined manners, and who does not attract the attention of the clientele. Thus, the men who come knocking at the door must be content at being received with minimal politeness, for the first woman they meet owes them no service. Moreover, to strip the man of his status of master of the harem, the director undermines his voyeuristic desire, by inviting him into the modern harem to find nary a woman giving into his visual fantasy, but rather a space where the man is liable to fill this role. When Nasser (Omar Bekhaled) shows up at the door of Zhor's property, Meriem rushes to the door not to be a serviceable maid but in hopes of coupling with him inside the gynaecium. Even though Nasser, who happens to be Sakina's suitor, reveals he is here to see Sakina, Meriem goes on to say: 'Qu'est-ce que tu es beau!' (Aren't you good-looking!).

Moknèche proposes to shatter the myth of the Odalisque, and to make the women of his harem play the role that they discern in the modern harem, freed from the laws of man. This conception is disturbing and threatens to upset the masculine spectator who, in the eyes of the servant, wants to be served by the women who intend to reverse the private order of the harem and the public configuration of a society that they have vowed to obstruct and (re)determine.[9]

Focus on the Libertine Harem

Moknèche calls into question the widely recognised idea that the harem is an exclusively closed space. To begin with, he brings his camera into the harem. One could argue that he 'steals a glance' to which he has no right. After all, the director is a man. Moknèche's endeavour could be equated to that of Eugène Delacroix's, as Algerian writer Assia Djebar beautifully shows in her *Women of Algiers in Their Apartment* (1999), for the Frenchman penetrates—in every sense of the word—the forbidden harem in order to later immortalise the stolen glance in his paintings. In the framework of the modern harem, however, it is the woman who invites men to visit her by calling them to cross into her habitat. Besides, in the film, the man does not gaze furtively from the threshold. Women frankly pose as models, the models of a new type of disclosed women. In fact, from the beginning of *Harem*, Meriem's voice invites us to penetrate (into) the harem: 'Ta'ali ya ghazali' (Come on in, sweetheart—literally: my gazelle). Even before the opening scene, the spectator can hear her sing during the opening credits, which scroll on a black screen, just before Meriem appears. Singing subversive lyrics, Meriem puts on her makeup as if to show from the beginning of the movie—which takes place at the entrance to the harem—both the project to seduce and the expression of a new identity. The spectator ventures onto the property of a woman with a new face: that of subversion. Paradoxically, Meriem opens up the harem, a space, which by nature is the most enclosed of spaces. Meriem, played by the Algerian actress Biyouna, 'entertains' men, in every sense of the word, in her modern harem characterised by its openness, whereas the traditional harem is strictly closed off to all strangers. In *Viva*, Papicha, played by the very same actress, plays the role of a former seductress.

The women of the Moknèchian harem exercise the liberty to receive whomever they want, and visits are often paid by men. Whether at Zhor's villa or the Debussy Pension, the doors of these harems are always open. The women of the harem do not stand idly by, submissively waiting for the arrival of men. They seek them out (Goussem goes to meet Anis at his job, and even in his home). They introduce men to the harem. They set up rendezvous. The making of a rendezvous depends entirely on the will of the female characters who accept or refuse to have a relationship with the strangers who popu-late their intimacy, as is shown in this dialogue between a young man and Goussem '—Tu me rends fou, j'aimerais te revoir.—Si je dis non, tu vas me tuer?—On ne tue pas les gens qu'on aime.—Alors, c'est non!' (—You drive me crazy. I'd like to see you again.—If I say no, you're going to kill me?—You don't kill the people you love.—Then, it's no!). The men must obey the message left on Fifi's voicemail 'Laissez-moi un p'tit message' (Leave me a brief message), which grants her the sole privilege to accept or ignore her callers' requests. Even Meriem, 'the Odalisque of the exterior', has this power. Sid-Ali is seen talking to Sakina's professor and suitor, at the doorstep. When Meriem comes home, she yells, running toward the stranger, 'Eh, là-bas, eh! Tu cherches quoi?' (Hey, there! What is it?). Sid-Ali vanishes inside the property letting Meriem take over the right to turn away visitors. Blocking the passage with her arm, she asks: 'Qu'est-ce que tu veux?' [...] Qui tu es, toi?' (What'd you want? [...] Who are you?). Because he refuses Meriem's dishonest proposition, the visitor is not welcome in her harem.

The Moknèchian sisterhood is composed of women who obliterate moral restrictions and taboos, as well as the customs of their society. The women of the modern harem take charge of their bodies to use them to rebellious ends. By having sex with a married man, Goussem sets herself up in opposition to the traditional duty of a woman who preserves her virginity until the wedding night. She takes possession of her body and indulges in her sexuality according to modern principles that are largely influenced by the West—the same West that flaunts the worth of perfect bodies exhibited on the beaches of Miami, which Goussem sees in a televised documentary. Just as she does with a stranger she meets in a nightclub, she uses her body to attract and to better reject the man she just has had sex with. As a matter of fact, as Anis tries to bring his hand close to Goussem's genital region, she pushes it away and stands up. The following dialogue takes place: '—Je suis puni?—Oui, oui!—Oh, Goussem! Goussem!' (—Am I punished?—Yes!—Oh, Goussem! Goussem!). It is no longer the body-capital of a virgin, who passively presents herself to her husband on the wedding bed. It is an Epicurean body that claims personal pleasure. It is one that takes charge, uses and dismisses men as a mere commodity. It is a body-spring-board toward emancipation. It is an enabler of change in gender roles and female status.

In reference to the documentary, Papicha jokes about having her breasts augmented in France. Her comment, while flippant, brings home the double-edged sword that is the belief of women exerting control through the body. If Papicha were to have this surgery, it could be interpreted as a manifestation of her control over her own body, particularly because, as a widow, the decision would not be taken with the blessing—or according to the demands—of a *wali*, or male guardian. It could also conceivably give her a measure of sexual 'power' over men, and would represent a threat to the patriarchal ordering of society.[10] And yet, she would literally be cutting her body in response to a perceived male sexual fantasy about seductive femininity. But Papicha rejects this aspect of western modernity. Directly after her joke, she and her daughter giggle about the roasted chicken that they could have for dinner, suggesting a connection between plastic surgery and the objectification and consumption of the (female) body as, literally, 'meat'.[11]

Papicha recognises the potential power of her body in gaining a measure of control over men, even though this 'control' is necessarily framed within the terms of male desire. Papicha exercises this principal when she goes to the town hall on her search for infor-mation about the owner of *Le Copacabana*. There, an old man on his lunch break fancies her. She takes advantage of his desire to ask him for the information that is crucial to her quest and leaves as soon as she succeeds, failing to set up the rendezvous he was hoping for as payment for his help. Papicha's dream is not to reward men's sexual phantasm. She continues to mourn the death of her husband, and is not sexually active. She does not aspire to conform totally to male expectations, but is willing to use her body as and when she chooses.

Similarly, Goussem makes tactical—and, arguably, equally problematic—use of her body in order to gain financial stability. She asks her boss, Mr. Mouffok, to give her permission to leave work early. It is the end of the month, payday, and she prepares Mr. Mouffok to hand over her check. However, he is not satisfied with the behaviour of his employee who is often late, absent and 'impolite to clients'. Goussem will not take 'no' for an answer, especially when it comes from a man. And even though she is fully aware of the poor quality of her work, Goussem uses her sexuality: she assumes a sensual tone and adds to the exoticism by making her request in English: 'Please, Mr. Mouffok. I wanna go out tonight. Mr. Mouffok, I wanna chic-chic-chic-a-boom-boom-boom all the night. Aw, please, Mr. Mouffok! Mr. Mouffok?' Mr. Mouffok finally obliges, he bows to her demands: he lets her leave work early and hands her the long-awaited envelope. She will not stop coming to work late and missing days under false pretexts: 'my mother slipped on a rock' or 'there was a terrorist attack'. Still, Mr. Mouffok does not sack her. While Goussem appears to persuade Mr. Mouffok to do her bidding, it is also apparent that her body represents an economic asset—in effect, an object of exchange—for his business. In the age of automatic photo booths, Samir, a young man who dreams of 'crossing the sea', and needs a passport photo, frequents Mr. Mouffok's shop in the hopes of flirting with Goussem, whom he follows around Algiers.

The Fall of the Anti-Hero

As Mernissi points out, women—contrary to popular belief—have effectively led men in certain Muslim countries, but their reign was not a pleasant one. The *Sitt* (Lady), states Mernissi, reigned either for a very short period, or anonymously under the cover of a man, or with the official recognition of a religious eminence, for the simple reason that power is a sacred subject, but it is also taboo, much like the harem. In the modern harem, man is dispossessed of his masculinity and consequently of his power. Indeed, when the daughter of Mme Osmane returns to the car to get the bouquet of flowers, a man worried that his wife is taking advantage of her moment of liberty to cheat on him accosts Sakina and asks her to make his wife come out: 'I don't want my wife hanging around men'. And Sakina reassures him: 'I tell you there are no men in there: a blind singer and a gay hairstylist, and that's it!' These two men are emasculated. Because they lost their *r'joulia* (Chebel, 1995, p. 199), these two characters become marginalised and thence are free to remain in the feminine space.

In Nadir Moknèche's films, the conventional structure of the harem has disappeared, but men occupy the place that they had previously assigned to women in the traditional harem. They are placed in a subaltern position where they are reduced to a simple utilitarian function that they can never seem to escape. Besides the singer and the hairdresser, there is also a jack-of-all-trades who serves Zhor in *Harem*, and a concierge at the service of the women of the Debussy Pension. The latter, always inside the four walls of the harem, often with his daughter in his arms, helps his spouse with housekeeping chores. One could argue that these men are examples of the ultra-modern version of the house-husband. Adrift in a power structure that supersedes them, they are pushed aside by the women, who take centre stage.

Singing and dancing in honour of the young bride and the girls of Bab el-Oued, the women celebrate a new era in the making, that of freer women. Following the lead of the female singer, they shout raising their fists in the air: 'Long live the girls from Bab el-Oued!' But in order to escape their fate, they must inaugurate a new regime, find new candidates to dominate a modern power structure. In *Harem*, the usual master has left the scene. He is in France, and has effectively relinquished his place. In his absence, the mistress automatically appoints herself to the vacant post. Since men have become less present, the women have decided to try their hand at leading.

The harem that wishes to subvert the order must disseminate the power among the women on the frontlines—not of *national* liberation, but of *feminine* liberation, in which men inherit vacant and meaningless roles at the interior of the harem and are resigned to the tasks that await them at home. The former oppressors find themselves constricted by an inversion of roles and spaces, which turns them into mere subalterns.

Reframing Space

On the way to the church, Sakina asks in a weary voice: 'Where's that fucking sea?' Almost instantaneously it appears on the horizon to the great joy of everyone who cries out: 'The sea!' Even before they arrive at the church, they begin to dance on the asphalt. They take possession of the road, exorcising death and confinement, letting the wind blow off their burden-headscarves that seem to form a chain between them, not of iron links, but symbolic of the traditional harem left behind and the modern harem that lies ahead. The movement takes place in a revelatory way: mixing Arab dance with western dress. Filmed from afar, these women are like the birds from the end of the film *Halfouine, l'enfant des terrasses* (*Halfouine: Boy of the Terraces*) (1990) in the background of the credits. They seem to move without restriction, not in the endless Tunisian sky, but against the immense blue of the Algerian seaside.[12] The Mediterranean Sea marks the absence of limits for the para-community of Moknèchian women. Here, like a pleasant surprise, the cool breeze coming off the sea brings liberation straight to the women's faces. This long-awaited discovery marks the end of a struggle against the symbolic stifling of the heat that they flee in search of the freeing winds of change. The singer Cheikha Rimitti, one of the first Algerian female marginalists in the Algerian music tradition to encourage the emancipation of women in her songs, teases out the conceptual link between the sea breeze and freedom in 'C'est fini, j'en ai marre' ('It Is Finished, I've Had Enough') (2005)[13]: 'Kul shi neqeblah, wa l'ghemma lla. J'en ai marre, j'en ai marre. J'en ai marre, j'en ai marre. Rih lebhar drebni . . .' (I can accept everything but confinement: no! I've had enough, I've had enough. I've had enough, I've had enough. The sea breeze has blown on me . . .). Once they have arrived at their destination, the portable harem has lost its *raison-d'être*; the women let themselves be joyfully 'denuded' by the wind amidst exorcising dance and mocking laughter, appropriating the outside that is no longer synonymous with danger or the space of men alone.

Despite the existence of a binary division of space in Algeria, women do not hesitate to join men outside to conquer the territory of the other gender. Sakina ventures to the car to get a bouquet of flowers, passing in front of two young men who whistle at her. She later beats one of them with her bag requesting that he let go of Kahina, whom she finds dancing with him and other guys. In the first phase of their marginalisation (forced marginalisation or peri-community), the feminine characters are enclosed in a dwelling where they hide from fundamentalists. Shortly, in the next phase (the para-community), determined to play a decisive role in the reclaiming of social space, the women infiltrate spaces traditionally frequented by men only, such as bars. These are occasions for the women to undo the classic configuration of space that consists in the traditional rigid partitioning, with men on one side in public (outside); and women in the private space (inside). Whereas the *marabout* lies in ruin, the Algerian youth carries itself voluntarily to give credit to a new Algeria by running the nightclubs, products of the modern era. Modernity, symbolised by *Le Paradoxe*, a club in Bouzaréah is preferred by the youth who make of it a paracommunitarian *marabout* or shrine. In fact, in *Viva*, the young people find themselves in a club, with dancing, drinking, flirting and dating. Men and women imitating the hip youth of the countries across the Mediterranean find themselves in a common space to share all sorts of modern pleasures from alcoholic drinks consumed at the bar listening to westernised Algerian music or Spanish pop, to sexual relations with strangers. The rules of separation of the sexes are obliterated. In fact, in the traditional harem structure, the man cannot access the private areas of the harem unless one of the women who occupy it shares a direct and legitimate familial relation with him through marriage or bloodline. In the modern harem, this is not the case. The public sphere is also that of women. The nightclub is Goussem's place of abandonment, and the cabaret is that of Papicha. There, they permit themselves to wholeheartedly engage in practices judged illicit or shameful: they dance and drink with strangers of the opposite sex. In these two places of dance, of alcoholic consumption, and of fleeting encounters, the separations between the sexes do not exist. I said earlier that the harem is both a sacred and prohibited place. The women indulge in practices that the mainstream society would qualify as sinful, or '*haram*' in Arabic. Therefore, it is by introducing the '*haram*' as 'sin' into the 'sacred' '*harim*' that women are able to end the traditional harem.

Rating: Graphic, Explicit, Provocative

Through this shift, the passage from forced to voluntary marginalisation takes place. Here, I must highlight, as odd as the expression 'voluntary marginalisation' may sound, that this is what it is about, for if power is to continue in a life of debauchery condemned by the moral discourse of the community, then women must make a conscious choice to endorse their very marginality, which becomes a sort of struggle for a new environment where the margin mutates into the norm and the norm is pushed to the side. In response to the politics of confinement, they are at the core of a politics of insubordination to men.

When literature and cinema portray the harem, they often represent a space where women share the love of a single man, and when the sexual aspect of the harem is evoked, one imagines the lewd and excessive sexual desires of the master, which women are required to attend to. The sexualised character of the harem implies a strict separation of the sexes, with women at the interior of the harem, desperately awaiting the arrival of the master.[14] In Moknèche's films, these stereotypes wash out and assume all the dimensions of a stereotype, for the case is just the opposite. In fact, the characters are women liberated to excess. Fifi is a prostitute, Papicha is a former bar girl, Meriem is an 'emancipated'[15] woman, and Yasmine, a young woman who travels across the Algerian countryside in a mini-skirt that shows her 'long legs' that 'will excite the [zealots]'

(Madame, avec ses grandes jambes, elle va les exciter). Moknèche's cinema puts liberated sexuality at the fore, in every sense of the word, representing it in an original and provocative way. One must see in the sex on the screen a subversive way of making spaces interpenetrate, the symbol of intrusion of the emancipated woman into the public sphere.

Above and beyond images of breasts on the verge of exploding from bodices, and the shortest western outfits on the market, women like Goussem and Fifi are shown naked. Goussem is filmed from the front in the nude, and Fifi appears in full frontal nudity as she exits the shower. These nude scenes occur after Goussem is shown having sex with married Anis and after Fifi made love with 'Chouchou', a police official. To take the provocation even further, these characters commit this carnal act with other men of their choosing.

The Disoriented Harem: or, Filming in French

In Moknèche's cinema, new practices and socio-cultural elements from the West take their place in the Algerian universe. In what respect do Papicha, Goussem, Sakina and Fifi appear to be westernised in these places? First of all, they speak French. This choice can be explained by what Assia Djebar says in *Fantasia: An Algerian Cavalcade* (1993) about the power of the French language, in as much as she lets it speak of her, of love, and of taboo subjects that are difficult to express in Arabic due to a certain *hchouma* ('chastity') attached to it. Algerian Arabic is a hybrid language, one that incorporates more Gallicisms and French than any other regions of the Maghrib. But Moknèche goes even further still. His films are not in Algerian but in French. The names of places are French so that Moknèche can Gallicise his world and disorient his public, making it easier to accept the depiction of his characters leading a westernised way of life in an Algeria always in contact with western elements. For example, the West is present in Algeria in the characters of a Russian collaborator (Mr. Stoliaroff) in *Harem*, and a Frenchman (Mr. Farès) in *Viva*, among others. In several instances, the foreign element grants the director the liberty in each of his films, to propose his vision of his country as the result of the remodelling of exclusively Maghribi structures in contact with the West.

Why choose to make the characters appear more French and less Algerian? According to the director and producer, the choice of language was a practical one: what other way to unite an Algerian-speaking cast with Lubna Azabal who speaks Moroccan Arabic?: 'faire parler Lubna Azabal dans sa langue, l'arabe marocain, serait ridicule' (to have Lubna Azabal speak in Moroccan Arabic, her language, would be ridiculous).[16] But Moroccan and Algerian Arabic are very similar. In some respect, it seems convenient to coach Azabal to express herself in Algerian for the sake of the movie.[17] It is a relatively common practice in the film industry, to have characters speak in a different accent with a different vocabulary for the sake of authenticity. Finally, the non-Arab-speaking public, which is significant, would get nothing but the light of the screen. In my opinion, besides the obvious marketing aspect, the director's choice of French must be explained as a means chosen to more easily emphasise the connection between Algeria and western cultures, and to help the spectator more readily accept his conception of the modern harem as both a domestic and national Algerian structure.

The Occidental qualities go beyond the use of the French language. In addition to relevant scenes of modern behaviour among Moknèche's cast, such as the ones showing Sakina smoking in public, extramarital relations and the consumption of alcohol are no doubt the influence of audiovisual programmes received through the satellite dish. These qualities are also of a meta-cinematographic nature. Carmen Maura, who plays the part of Madame Osmane, is a Spanish actress. She is 'una chica Almodóvar' (one of Almodóvar's girls) as described by the media in her country. It is easier to redress a structure firmly grounded in society (the harem) by removing it from its context, by denaturalising it and strengthening the effects of foreign elements. The fact that Maura is a Spaniard helps one to accept an Occidental woman at the head of a harem. A French figure could have led to an outrageous amalgamation, the depiction of a re-colonisation of Algerian society and the involvement of the former empire into the affairs of the nation. Thus the notion of a 'de-algerianisation', a modern harem in an Algeria plagued by an internal fissure between tradition and modernity, is more conceivable in a deterritorialised universe.

The Moknèchian harem is a hybrid entity because of the Occidental influence at its interior: Spanish with Maura, *beur* with the presence of Yasmine,[18] French by the choice of the language[19] and the nationality of the film crew and certain actors, Moroccan with Azabal and the shooting location (*Harem* was filmed in Morocco for security reasons). Paradoxically, it is further modernised by the participation of Biyouna, an inspirational character from Algerian national television, and a 'chica Moknèche' (since she plays a role—as well as Nadia Kaci—in both films by 'the Algerian Almodóvar', and plays another in *Délice Paloma*). For the Maghribi and *Beur* audiences, she symbolises the woman with 'modern ideas': the woman who 'drinks', who dares to denounce the status of women in Algeria and who proclaims loud and long her desire to see the reformation of Algerian social structures.

THE END ... of the Traditional Harem and the Modern Harem ... To Be Continued

Benjamin Stora defines the Moknèchian cinema thusly: 'Le cinéma de Nadir Moknèche quelque part, c'est un cinéma aussi qui nous dit les mutations d'une société, c'est-à-dire une société qui est en situation de bascule et c'est ça qui donne, disons, cette espèce de virulence dans les attitudes, d'inquiétudes aussi, d'agressivité parce qu'il montre une bascule, je veux dire un moment charnière dans une société'. (The cinema of Nadir Moknèche in some ways, is also a cinema which tells us of the mutations of society, which is to say a society that is in a situation of shift, and this is what gives us, let's say, a kind of virulence in the attitudes, a kind of worry, too, an aggression because it shows a shift, I mean, a pivotal moment in society.) *Le Harem de Mme Osmane* and *Viva Laldjérie* illustrate the conflicted character of the hopes of some for tradition and others for modernity in a contemporary Algeria that is in a state of change. This society is composed of a population in which the majority is under the age of 25. Scarred by a heavy past, which television, newspapers and political discourses will not forget, the unemployment that transforms young men into *hittistes*, the estrangement of Europe that is closing off its borders, the Algerian youths like Samir have, at worst, only a fabricated dream of escape to offer themselves; at best, a long struggle to wage against the traditional structures of the nation. These two films depict an Algeria which, with the impetus of women and despite all the hurdles, transgresses taboos, engages a new way of life and fights against numerous obstacles. It is an Algeria that is making itself a future with the tools that it has at its disposal. The director gives us the modern harem, an allegory of an Algerian nation that, as Stora points out, is not used to seeing itself 'involved in social, cultural and economic modernisation'. This reconstitution of an Algerian politics of space in contact with the West is pervasive even in the title of the second film. 'Laldjérie' is an idiom inspired by a slogan shouted in stadiums: 'One, two, three ... Viva Lalgérie'. Moknèche recognises the existence of this 'contraction' between 'el-Dzajaïr', which 'is already a bit heavy' and 'l'Algérie, which is French', a contraction that shows that 'there is something that is not working in [Algerian] identity'. This slogan, at once Gallicised and Anglicised, is a testimony of the hope of the younger generation to propose their own identity, and is women's motto. Neither entirely 'Algérie' nor 'Djazaïr', 'Laldjérie' is a social, cultural and linguistic *bricolage*, its differences driven by an opening of the actual world unto a world that is new, western, in a (Maghribi) word, modern. Moknèche's message is clear: women are the future of Algeria. Does Moknèche's third film not have as a main character a woman named 'Madame Aldjéria'? In spite of their most unenviable fate, Algerian women have always taken the fate of the country into their own hands during belligerent times. They have embraced it. They have empathised with it without condition. Moknèche's films are his homage to all the brave and anonymous Madames Aldjéria.

Acknowledgements

The author would like to express his thanks and appreciation to Greta Bliss, Daniel Brewer, Brian Edwards, Isaac Joslin, Andrea Khalil, Nasrin Qader, Mireille Rosello, Altoni Shackelford and Robert St. Clair for their valuable contributions, and to Kamel, Yakhlef and Zahra Abderrezak, Hayate, Ib Tissem and Ilyess Arbi and Faïza, Inès and Yanis Jellad for their love and support.

Notes

1. The Interview can be found in the French package made of two DVDs, which does not provide English subtitles. In my chapter, I will be referring to the French version of *Viva Laldjérie*. English translations for this film are my own. For *Le Harem de Mme Osmane*, English translations are from the DVD's subtitles.
2. Moknèche's third feature film. *Délice Paloma* began French distribution in July 2007. The following synopsis is available online from http://www.unifrance.org. 'Madame Aldjéria, with her team, fixes up other people's problems in exchange for cash. She doesn't hesitate to dirty her hands in order to survive in a country where no holds are barred. Paloma, her new recruit, catches everyone's eye, beginning with Riyad, Aldjéria's son. Madame Aldjéria is on a deal close to her heart: buying the Caracalla Thermae. But this is one deal too much, too grandiose; becausee [*sic*] of it she losses her son and her freedom'.
3. Nadir Moknèche spent many years abroad. From 1993 to 1995 he studied cinema at the New School for Social Research in New York and made two short films, one of which was the award-winning *Hanifa, ainsi va l'amour* (a modern adaptation of the myth of Medea). His portrayal of modern woman (or, the intersections of women/femininity and modernity) has been central to this work since his first project.
4. It does in Modern Standard Arabic (MSA) too, as the *Hans Wehr Dictionary* (Cowan) (1993) shows. In this lexicon, one can find the following words as translations of 'modern' or *'asri*, as it is called in MSA: 'recent, present, actual, contemporary, modernist'.
5. See, for example, Leïla Sebbar's short story 'La Jeune fille au balcon' in the collection by the same name.
6. My emphasis.
7. One should note that in Gillo Pontecorvo's film *The Battle of Algiers* (1966), it is bombs that women carry in their baskets while they are wearing the *haïk*. In *Viva*, Fifi uses her cell phone as a weapon against traditional Algeria. At the same time, it enables her to keep in touch with modernity.

8. This is a neologism that I contruct from *'dışarı'*, which means 'outside' in Turkish.
9. The character of the revolted maid who cheats, threatens, endangers, etc. the (head of the) household has become a very popular topic of T.V. serials in the Maghrib. This is the sign that Maghribis have become aware of a drastic change in power relations in their harems.
10. As *The Battle of Algiers* suggests, a woman's body, when unveiled, is a body ready to attack. In the struggle for liberation, the unveiling was offered to the nationalist cause, against the foreigner. In the modern harem, the body is brandished against men and their traditional rules.
11. Moreover, she does not take seriously the idea of going to France to see the other *Copacabana* opened by a group of exiled Algerians in memory of the cabaret by the same name, that closed in Algiers in 1993, for Papicha confides to the concierge that she would never 'sink so low as to request a visa from the French'.
12. On the subject of child para-community in Férid Boughedir's film, see my article *'Halfouine, l'enfant des terrasses* : L'individu - oiseau face à la communauté' published in the summer 2006 special issue of *Expressions maghrébines* on Tunisia.
13. My transliteration and translation.
14. This is the case in the Tunisian films *Samt el qusur* (*The Silences of the Palace*) (1994) and *La Saison des hommes* (*The Season of Men*) (2000).
15. This is how Goussem is qualified on the cover of the DVD distributed by the company Film Movement.
16. Moknèche explains the choice of language in a conversation with Benjamin Stora at http://www.commeaucinema.com/news.php3?nominfos=27383&Rub=Notes.
17. As a matter of fact, Azabal was coached to speak some Spanish in the film *Exils* (*Exiles*) (2004).
18. *'Beur'* is a term used to designate a French citizen of Maghribi descent; it is the inversion of the Arabic word meaning 'Arab'.
19. In April 2004, during the press conference in Algiers that followed the release of *Viva* in Algeria, Moknèche was harshly criticized for his choice of French over the 'Francarabe' of Algiers. This led many critics to question the 'Algerianness' of Moknèche's cinema.

References

Abderrezak, H. (2006) *'Halfouine, l'enfant des terrasses*: L'individu-oiseau face à la communauté', *Expressions maghrébines* 5(1), pp. 83–96.
'Algeria's Women Quietly Advance in Careers and Society' *The New York Times on the Web*, 25 May 2007 at <http://www.nytimes.com/2007/05/25/world/africa/25cnd-algeria.html?ex=1337745600&en=de718f38a>.
Alloula, M. (1986) *The Colonial Harem*, trans. M. Godzich and W. Godzich, Minneapolis, University of Minnesota Press.
Bab el-Oued City (1994) Directed by Merzak Allouache.
The Battle of Algiers (1966) Directed by Gillo Pontecorvo.
'C'est fini, j'en ai marre' (2005) In *The Essential Guide to Arabia*, London, Union Square Music.
Certeau, M. de (1984) *The Practice of Everyday Life*, trans. S.F. Rendall, Los Angeles, University of California Press.
Chebel, M. (1995) *L'Esprit de sérail: Mythes et pratiques sexuels au Maghreb*, Paris, Payot.
Cowan, J.M. (Ed.) (1993) *Hans Wehr Dictionary of Modern Written Arabic*, Urbana, Spoken Language Services.
Délice Paloma (2007, forthcoming) Directed by Nadir Moknèche.
Djebar, A. (1993) *Fantasia: An Algerian Cavalcade*, trans. D.S. Blair, Portsmouth, Heinemann.
Djebar, A. (1999) *Women of Algiers in Their Apartment*, trans. M. de Jager, Charlottesville, University of Virginia Press.
Edwards, B.T. (2005) *Morocco Bound: Disorienting America's Maghreb, from Casablanca to the Marrakech Express*, Durham, NC, Duke University Press.
Encyclopedia of Islam (1960) Leiden, Brill.
Exils (2004) Directed by Tony Gatlif.
Halfaouine—Boy of the Terraces (1990) Directed by Férid Boughedir.
Hanifa, ainsi va l'amour (1994) Directed by Nadir Moknèche.
Le Harem de Mme Osmane (2000) Directed by Nadir Moknèche.
Leclère, T. (2004) Entretien avec le réalisateur, *Télérama* 2830, <http://www.abc-lefrance.com/fiches/vivalaldjerie.pdf>.

Mernissi, F. (1993) *The Forgotten Queens of Islam*, trans. M.J. Lakeland, Minneapolis, University of Minnesota Press.

La Saison des hommes (2000) Directed by Moufida Tlatli.

Samt el qusur (1994) Directed by Moufida Tlatli.

Sebbar, L. (2001) *La Jeune fille au balcon*, Paris, Points.

Stora, B. (2004) Interview entre Benjamin Stora et Nadir Moknèche, <http://www.commeaucinema.com/news.php3?nominfos=27383&Rub=Notes>.

Viva Laldjérie (2004) Directed by Nadir Moknèche.

Ali Zaoua: The Harsh Life of Street Children and the Poetics of Childhood

JOSEF GUGLER

Ali Zaoua: Prince of the Streets, set in Casablanca, is the story of four boys who have broken away from a gang of street children that is ruled by an abusive older boy, Dib. Ali, his best friend Kwita, and Omar have just reached puberty, while Boubker is a few years younger. During a confrontation with the gang, Ali is killed by a stone. His three friends decide to bury him, 'like a prince'.

Nabil Ayouch[1] presents fine psychological portrayals of his child protagonists, even if they appear rather naive at times. Working with street children, he succeeded in eliciting performances to match the realities of the children in spite of the formidable difficulties he encountered. The technical qualities of his production are remarkable: cinemascope takes full advantage of a principal location that offers a nearly 360 degree view of the harbour and the city; extended takes are employed effectively; the animation sequences are delightful.

Ali Zaoua was a big success in Morocco. Selling close to 500,000 tickets, it eclipsed all previous Moroccan productions, except for a few comedies. Quite likely it was the most successful film from anywhere in the Maghrib. Internationally it has been the most

Figure 1. Ali and his friends

successful Moroccan film ever (Dwyer, 2005), garnering 44 prizes in international festivals, according to Ali N'Productions, Ayouch's production company. The film's numerous prizes include the Stallion of Yennenga, the Grand Prize, at the premier festival of African film, FESPACO (Panafrican Film and Television Festival of Ouagadougou). In the US it found distribution as a selection of the Film Movement subscription series.[2] Critical comment, however, has remained limited.

Filming with Street Children

The film's opening sequence, when Ali, for the benefit of a television reporter, invents a story about his mother preparing to sell his eyes, may be taken as a comment on Ayouch's experience when he embarked on this film. At first he had gone into the streets with a camera, but he soon found that the children were adept at telling what they assumed outsiders wanted to hear. Ayouch quickly abandoned his camera and ended up spending two years becoming familiar with the children. He received crucial assistance from Dr Najat M'jid, the founder and president of Bayti, an NGO devoted to child welfare, and her collaborators.[3]

Ali and his three friends were street children.[4] Except for Omar, who had a big scar added for his performance, the four friends were already scarred when Ayouch met them; indeed their scars were much less remarkable than what Ayouch had come to see during those two years preparing the film. Abdelhak Zhayra, in the role of Ali, came from Fez. Ayouch had met him near the train station late one evening. He was struck by Zhayra's proud look. They had sandwiches then, but did not meet again until a chance encounter several months later. When Ayouch told Zhayra of Ali's dreams, they appeared to be close to the boy's own. Once Zhayra had joined the set, it came as a disappointment to him that his role was rather brief even though his Ali Zaoua was giving the film its name.

Mounïm Khab was also from Fez. Ayouch still had not found the boy to play Kwita when he met him five days before the beginning of the shooting. It was Khab who approached Ayouch, who told him about the film and recruited him in short order. Khab had spent some time as a carpenter's apprentice, and he found it hard to pretend incompetence when working with Mohamed Majd, aka Hamid, the fisherman.

Ayouch had met Mustapha Hansali when he visited the wholesale market in the company of an educator one night. When asked to improvise a situation, he revealed himself to be an extraordinarily sensitive child. Hansali had a difficult relationship with his mother, and it was hard for him to take on the role of Omar *vis-à-vis* Ali's mother. Also, he did not want to be filmed in the nude while Ali's mother bathed him. Amal Ayouch finally persuaded him, explaining how much more difficult it had been for her, married, with two children, to simulate sex with a client.

After Ayouch had seen Hicham Moussoune at Bayti, he told his co-writer Nathalie Saugeon that they absolutely had to include this child who was always joking and had an incredible smile. When she in turn looked him up, he volunteered to sing, and sang so well that they decided that he definitely would have to sing in the film. Thus Boubker came to provide cheer for his comrades and humour for viewers, all this cheer even though Moussoune had lost his mother just before the shooting began. He was the only one who wanted to become an actor, and he appeared set to realise his ambition: he went on to a television series and a major role in Ayouch's next film, *A Minute of Sun Less*.

Some of the boys in Dib's gang, including Dib's right-hand man Khalid, were also street children Ayouch had come to know during those two years preparing the film. However, most of Dib's gang lived in an orphanage. Thirty members of the gang appear in the credits. Noureddine, aka Winston, was indeed a cigarette seller from the harbour, where he was known by everybody.

Figure 2. Nabil Ayouch directing Boubker, Omar, and Kwita

Ayouch (2001; Lowry, 2001) has dwelt on the difficulty of working with street children. They could not adapt to the requirements of filming, and the attempt to adapt the filming to the children did not work either. Furthermore, there were conflicts between the children, as well as between the children and Saïd Taghmaoui, in the role of the gang leader Dib, who arrived as an established actor.[5] Only after two or three weeks, when everybody became convinced of the usefulness of the film, did things fall into place. At the end of the shooting Hicham Moussoune, the benjamin of the foursome, began to cry, and nearly everybody else joined in. A major complication arose early on because Mouniïm Khab, in the role of Kwita, fell madly in love with Nadia Ould Hajjaj, who was playing the high school student, the very first day they acted together. His infatuation caused the shooting to be suspended for five weeks: after a shoot he ran to impress his love, jumped over a low wall, and fell into a 15 foot deep hole, breaking his foot. He drew the flowers on the wall next to her, and added little hearts below—the film shows one of them.

Dr Najat M'jid and her collaborators at Bayti were closely involved with the children from the very beginning. The children were told that this was only a stage in their life. Not only did they gain assurance from the experience, some rejoined their families, returned to school, invested their earnings in micro-projects or professional training (Ayouch, 2001; Barlet, 2003; M'jid, 2001; Saugeon, 2001b).

The Portrayal of Street Life

Ali Zaoua depicts the harshness and precariousness of the life of street children. The boys steal, prostitute themselves, sniff glue and have murderous fights with each other; they get raped by other boys; they are chased by the police. The children use a language of the streets that is considered rather vulgar, and many Moroccans were shocked by it—the English and French subtitles fail to do it justice (Barlet, 2003). Nevertheless, the reality presented in *Ali Zaoua* is rather gentle when compared to the grim representations of street children in classics such as Bunuel's *Los Olvidados*, Brazil's *Pixote* and *City of God* and India's *Salaam Bombay!* If Ali gets killed such was not the intent of the boy throwing a stone at him. To some extent this contrast may reflect differences between these settings. The armed youth gangs of Brazil presumably are not found in Morocco. Police systematically killing street children has only been reported from Brazil. Still, when Saugeon (2001b), who had worked on the scenario in France, came to Morocco for the first time, she was shocked to discover that the conditions of street children were harsher and more violent than their script allowed. At that point Ayouch told her that they were not doing a documentary, that there are things that cannot be put into a narrative film.

Ali Zaoua is moving, touching, indeed enchanting. The children find companionship with each other, troubled though it is. Kwita's encounter with a puppy may be taken as emblematic of the relations among the boys. Like the boys who fight and seek companionship, so Kwita repeatedly throws the puppy down a stairway, but the puppy keeps coming back and eventually settles around Kwita's neck. Ayouch transcends the harsh reality of street life altogether with a poetics of childhood.[6] He has argued in an interview that this poetics is part of street life:

The street holds a strong attraction, it has also a form of poetry and of a nearly tragical-lyric dreamworld that is difficult to imagine if one is not there, if one

Figure 3. The Island of the Two Suns

does not live there. Their life is made of deliriums, of phantasms coming from nowhere. They take off from anything, they have that poetry in themselves which is very strong and constitutes a pillar of their existence and helps them manage.[7] (Barlet, 2003)

Ayouch's Ali has created a veritable dream world of journeying on a boat, taking a girl aboard, and reaching the Island of the Two Suns. Eventually his friends get drawn into that dream world as well. The children, used to sniffing glue and escaping their reality, now see images on billboards and graffiti transform and become part of Ali's story. His magnificent mural painting of that island, which eventually becomes animated, and the animated designs of the boys' daydreams, the handiwork of Sylvie Leonard, are delightful.

Nathalie Saugeon (2001a), who had co-authored the script with Nabil Ayouch, wrote a novella of *Ali Zaoua* for young teens in French. *Ali Zaoua, prince de la rue* follows the film closely. However, the scene of Ali's mother having sex with a customer, and the allusions to rape and to the prostitution of Kwita, were dropped.

A painting and animation conveyed Ali's dreams and phantasy in the film in an enchanting fashion, but the novella foregoes all illustration. Saugeon succeeded, even without the poetics of images, in movingly conveying how the children's imagination transcends their harsh reality. The ending takes the burial party into Ali's dream world as Hamid, with the three boys and Ali's mother, sets course for the open sea. When Boubker from the mast sees, or perhaps just imagines, land in the far distance, Hamid sets Ali's little boat out on the water. As Kwita, the narrator, tells it:

And then something incredible happened. Something I will never forget. The wind rose brutally and it barged into the sail of the small boat. Boubker shouted. He who had made it, who had fixed that piece of cloth with his own hands, now saw an immense sail blowing up as he was looking.
The sail boat was propelled into the distance.
Evening was coming. Suddenly, in the distance, I saw a minute piece of land confounded with the horizon.
I said to Hamid:

—Look! There is an island!

—What did I tell you! screamed Boubker, overexcited.

Mrs Zaoua looked at us, then she squinted in the distance. She also saw it, she had a suggestion of a smile. (Saugeon, 2001a, p. 101)

The novella concludes with a coda taking readers back to reality. They learn that Kwita is an apprentice carpenter. He wants to become a carpenter, and he is just as determined as Ali had been to pursue his vocation. Like the novella, the film appears to end in Ali's dream world, but it also takes the viewer back to reality as they get one last look at the boys' abode on the edge of the harbour. Ayouch (2001) has commented that he felt the need to get back to reality, that this return, and the sun and the moon coming together for the first time like the two suns in Ali's dream, conveyed hope.

The Avoidance of Social Critique

Ali Zaoua is a new departure for Moroccan film, and indeed Arab film,[8] in focusing on street children, in conveying a good deal about their condition, in going so far as to allude to them prostituting themselves and being raped by other children. But if Ayouch brings attention to a social problem, he stays clear of social critique.[9]

In this film's telling, poverty is not at issue. We see the children on an old quay, on an abandoned factory site, on an empty lot, but only once can we catch a brief glimpse of shanties. Beyond the street children, we do not encounter poverty. The prostitution of Ali's mother is quite removed from the more sordid variations of the trade. She picks up her clients at a nightclub and takes them to her apartment. She appears to enjoy a modest level of comfort. Poverty did not drive Ali into the streets. *Ali Zaoua* starts out with a television reporter interviewing Ali. He tells of his mother preparing to sell his eyes. Ali is street smart and knows how to impress. The interviewer is taken in, and so are viewers until they learn the real reason Ali left home and come to know his mother. He ran away from home because he could not support children taunting his mother about her occupation.[10] His mother's comment 'You kids are cruel!' holds the children responsible for their condition. The film does not tell how any of the other children came to live in the streets. If we do not hear of poverty, there is no mention of family conflicts either; at most there may be a hint: as little Boubker keeps talking about his caring uncle, we hear his friends' dismissive rejoinders, see his scarred face, and begin to wonder whether mistreatment brought him to join the street children. The concluding song, 'Come my dear son/Come under my wings', tells of parents ready to welcome them to homes with 'green gardens, embedded with flowers and roses'—as if it were a perfectly simple choice to make, and a most attractive one at that.[11]

As for the treatment of street children, there is no indication of what they might endure at the hands of unsympathetic adults. Most people literally overlook them. Kwita repeatedly seeks to approach a high school student, but she virtually ignores him—they live in separate worlds. When street children do manage to connect with others, they are put down. Ali's mother berates Omar and his friends for their personal hygiene and for sniffing glue. The three friends followed Muslim injunction in washing Ali's body and wanting to bury him the very next day, but when Kwita meets an age mate at the cemetery, he is told that he and his friends are not pure because of their lack of religious practice, that Ali cannot be buried at the cemetery because of his impurity—which, it seems, could be overcome if they had the money to pay for the burial. The children are ignored or put down, but we witness no repression. The three friends perceive their neighbour having the feet of a camel, the witch Aicha of the popular imagination, and she complains to the police about the racket they make in the middle of the night. The police officers, however, never catch up with the children, and we do not learn what treatment they might mete out.

All the people who come into contact with the children are kind. The two principal adult protagonists care a great deal about the children. Ali's mother cares not only for her child, but she eventually takes Omar into her home. The fisherman Hamid was going to hire Ali as his assistant, keeps looking for him when he disappears, gives him the decent burial his friends cannot manage, and in the end takes on Kwita. The meeting between Kwita and the boy at the cemetery ends on a conciliatory, inclusive note when the boy, as an afterthought, makes a final comment about Kwita's dead friend: 'You find him up there praying with the angels'. And while the high school student never talks to Kwita, her face and demeanour suggest a kind person, and she gives him a little smile at their last encounter.

Ali Zaoua puts the blame for the condition of the street children squarely on them: on the children who tease Ali about his mother's profession; on Ali who lets himself be shamed into running away from home and confronts Dib's entire gang to defend her honour; on a gang member who fells him with a stone; on children who turn violent, most dramatically when Omar sets out to cut Kwita's throat. In this story it remains for children to take the initiative to escape their condition: Ali was committed to become a sailor and persuaded, we presume, Hamid to take him on as an assistant; Omar seeks out Ali's mother.

If the motivations of these children are innocent enough, the gang leader Dib may be readily perceived as simply evil: a young man who ruthlessly seeks to impose his will on younger children, and who rapes little Boubker along the way. But a closer look raises intriguing questions. Dib is a brutal leader indeed, but that begs the question how he has come to have 30-odd boys follow him. Apart from his right-hand man Khalid who articulates what he can only mumble and gesticulate, and perhaps a few boys hanging around him, we do not see the hierarchical structure that would allow him to control such a large body of independent-minded boys. And there is no suggestion that the band operates *en masse* to secure resources; rather we see individuals surrendering to Dib what they obtained on their own. We may conclude that Dib effectively looks

Figure 4. Dib and his gang

after his followers. Indeed one sequence shows Dib feeding one of the boys unable to eat on his own.

As for the personality of this gang leader, he is most unusual. Deaf and near mute, Dib is anything but a normal adult. We can only guess at the trauma related to his condition, but there are hints of a character more complex than the 'evil' label implies. He appears to feel remorse for the killing of Ali, accidental as it was. When he learns that Ali's friends plan to have him buried, he has the boy who threw the deadly stone dig a grave. And we are left to wonder about his expression, and his attempt to communicate, as Ali's mother comes to find her dead son.

Whatever the nuances, the overall thrust of *Ali Zaoua* is clear-cut. The life of street children in Casablanca is hard and precarious. No adults are to blame. No social policy, or lack thereof, comes ever into play. The blame rests on children running wild and a severely handicapped gang leader. *Ali Zaoua* has viewers conclude that the causes of Ali becoming a street child are fortuitous, that the only harm the street children experience is brought on by other children, if it is not self-inflicted. We are left not to address the causes of kids becoming street children and their condition, but to sympathise with them and to educate them. The film offers individual solutions to the social problem as Omar seeks out Ali's mother and Kwita works with Hamid and they take the boys under their wings.

Censorship, Funding, and Audiences

Self-censorship may go a long way to explain why Ayouch toned down the reality of the life of street children and avoided social critique.[12] *Ali Zaoua* was shot about the time Hassan II died, bringing to a close a long period of fierce repression of all opposition that has come to be referred to as the Years of Lead. If the political context may well explain why Ayouch avoided social critique, it also suggests that we be alert to subtle clues to subversive intent. It then becomes tempting to interpret the story of Dib's autocratic rule of his gang, and of the four friends who endure persecution when they try to break away, as an allegory for Moroccan politics: an autocratic King who is deaf and dumb, and progressive politicians who are persecuted. If they are ignored by most people, put down by others, there is also a good deal of sympathy for them. Eventually even the followers of Dib/the King join in their chant mourning Ali. In the end we are left to wonder to what extent Dib has changed, as Hassan II did to some extent in the last years of his reign.

Apart from outright censorship, we may further surmise that the French television networks who invested in the film, and the Moroccan, French, Belgian, and European agencies who contributed to the financing, would have balked at supporting a shocking film such as *Pixote* or *City of God*.[13] It is probably also the case that European and Moroccan audiences are not as inured to violence as those in the Americas.

While the violence of the streets remains limited in *Ali Zaoua*, the film is notably venturesome in other respects. Not only is a prostitute a principal protagonist, but Ali's mother is portrayed in very positive terms. As for her trade, she comments on children taunting her and Ali: 'I could have answered them. What could I tell them? Why their fathers come to me? You can't tell children that'. She is shown having sex with a client, a sequence on which, as Ayouch (2001) put it wryly, 'a lot of ink was spilt in Morocco'. Showing Omar frontally in the nude was also problematic. Ayouch touches on other sensitive topics as well, Boubker being raped by Dib, references to Kwita and other boys having been gang-raped by other boys, to Kwita prostituting himself, but he does it in a manner sufficiently subtle that they are unlikely to be picked up by young audiences. The success of the film certainly demonstrates that Ayouch made savvy choices.

Conclusion

In the context of Arab cinema, Nabil Ayouch's *Ali Zaoua, Prince of the Streets* breaks new ground in presenting the world of street children. At the same time his portrayal of their world stands in distinct contrast to that offered by classic representations emanating from other regions. If the vulnerability of children is central to the condition of street children, violence in *Ali Zaoua* remains limited and originates within their own ranks. Neither public authorities nor individual adults victimise these children; rather adults sympathetic to the children are shown helping them escape their condition.

The street life Ayouch portrays is harsh and precarious, but he avoids *miserabilism* by giving play to a poetics of childhood that finds expression in the daydreams of the children. Going to great length to recruit street children, he succeeded in eliciting performances that give psychological depth to his protagonists. The excellent cinemascope production is enhanced by delightful animation sequences of the children's dreams. Ayouch created a beautiful and enchanting film that emotionally engages viewers and elicits their sympathy for the condition of street children, all the while eschewing social critique.

Ali Zaoua was seen by close to half a million people in Morocco. If it affected the attitudes of some, if it moved them to act differently, it will have served a good purpose. Ayouch (2001), for one, has stated that public attitudes to street children changed a good deal since the film. He shall have the last word:

> Putting forward all the sentiments we share with them, universal sentiments, love, joy, fraternity, humor. Somehow making them more human in the eyes of people, and that is what happened when the film was released in Morocco. Many people were taken aback: 'we did not know that'. Inevitably, they now look at these children differently. There has been a debate, a polemic ensued which demonstrated that the film was the beginning of a new consciousness. (Barlet, 2003)

Acknowledgements

The author wishes to thank Andrea Khalil for helpful comments on an earlier version. The still of Ali and his friends is reproduced courtesy of Nabil Ayouch. The other illustrations are frames from *Ali Zaoua* and from the 'Making of' supplement on the French DVD.

Notes

1. Nabil Ayouch was born in France, the son of a Moroccan father and a French mother. For many years he spent half his time in Morocco, and he moved there recently (Barlet, 2003). This is his second full-length feature. His successful first one, *Mektoub*, has been described as a thriller, but the story of a couple who deal with the trauma of the rape she suffered suggests that there is more to it.
2. The DVD distributed in the US does not include the important supplementary materials provided on the French DVD: a running commentary on the film by Nabil Ayouch, a 'Making of' by Ayouch and the

actor Saïd Taghmaoui, a presentation of the characters by co-writer Nathalie Saugeon, and comments on the production by the producer Jean Cottin and Saugeon. The French DVD also offers English subtitles: they are more satisfactory and, in white, less jarring than the yellow subtitles on the US DVD.

3. Dr Najat M'jid has a cameo appearance as a car driver who rejects the bracelet offered by Boubker—of course she knows him full well.

4. The discussion of the recruitment of the child actors and their backgrounds relies largely on Ayouch (2001) and Saugeon (2001c).

5. Saïd Taghmaoui, familiar to US audiences from his role in *Three Kings*, is the best known of the professional actors Ayouch recruited for nearly all the adult roles. Ali's mother was played by Amal Ayouch, a cousin of the director, because it would have been very difficult for other Moroccan actresses to appear as a prostitute. Mohamed Majd, the fisherman Hamid, had appeared in foreign films produced in the studios of Southern Morocco; he went on to play the lead in Ayouch's *A Minute of Sun Less*. Nadia Ould Hajjaj, the high school student, subsequently became the national finalist for the world contest 'Elite Model Look' and got into modelling.

6. There are striking parallels between *Ali Zaoua* and Egyptian director Oussama Fawzi's *The Paradise of the Fallen Angels*, released the year before. In Cairo a middle-aged man abandons his bourgeois family to join a street society of pimps and prostitutes. When he dies of an overdose, his family recovers the body and prepares it for a respectable funeral, that is, to erase any trace of his street life. But his companions steal the body, and his daughter acquiesces that he did want to be with them. His friends take him on a final bout of drinking, card games and fighting that concludes on a fantastic trip. Companionship and ghoulish humour do not manage to lighten the persuasive gloom of street life in *Fallen Angels Paradise*. This contrasts with the approach of Nabil Ayouch who transcends the harshness and cruelty of the street children's life by introducing viewers to their dream world.

7. Translations from the French are mine.

8. Some Arab films focus on child labour, e.g. Hakim Noury's *L'Enfance volée*, Nouri Bouzid's *Clay Dolls*, but I am not aware of any devoted to street children.

9. The film did illustrate how readily hardware stores supply glue to children, and in its wake the government issued an ordinance restricting the sale of glue to children.

10. The revelation that Ali was adroitly playing to the sensationalist bent of much journalism is funny, but this exposure of the superficiality all too common in journalism also discounts the important role journalists do play in exposing suffering and injustice, and it undercuts any social critique—had Ali's story been for real, it would have highlighted poverty as a principal issue of children ending up on the streets, and it would have introduced the topic of the organ trade, a scourge of our times.

11. The maudlin lyrics of the song are not translated into either French or English on the French DVD.

12. Likewise in the women's shelter featured in Farida Ben Lyzaid's *A Door to the Sky*, produced a couple of years earlier, all explanation of the women's ordeal is limited to the personal circumstances of one woman who seeks refuge: '... [her husband] has just changed'.

13. Commenting on new developments in Moroccan cinema in the 1990s, Ayouch observed: 'When UGC [a French production company] or TF1 or Canal Plus [French television networks] agree to co-produce a film on the basis of the scenario, the proposed scenario is certainly not accepted as is, because those who invest in the film subsequently demand modifications and that also requires a great deal of work' (Samie, 2001).

References

Ali Zaoua, Prince of the Streets/Ali Zaoua, prince de la rue (2000) Directed by Nabil Ayouch, written by Nathalie Saugeon and Nabil Ayouch. Produced by Playtime (France), TF1 International (France), Ali N'Productions (Morocco), Alexis Films (Belgium), Ace Editing (Belgium). Distributed in the US by Arab Film Distribution and Film Movement.

Ayouch, N. (2001) Film commenté, on the French DVD of *Ali Zaoua*.

Barlet, O. (2003) Entretien avec Nabil Ayouch à propos de *Ali Zaoua*, <www.Africultures.com>.

City of God/Cidade de Deus (2002) Directed by Fernando Meirelles and Katia Lund, written by Braulio Mantovani.

Clay Dolls/Poupées d'argile/Arais al tein (2002) Written and directed by Nouri Bouzid.

A Door to the Sky/Bab Al-Sama Maftuh (1998) Written and directed by Farida Ben Lyzaid. Produced by France Media (France), Satipec (Tunisia), Interfilm (Morocco). Distributed in the US by Arab Film Distribution.

Dwyer, K. (2005) Personal communication.

L'Enfance volée (1993) Written and directed by Hakim Noury.

Los Olvidados (1950) Directed by Luis Buñuel, written by Luis Alcoriza and Luis Buñuel.

Lowry, S. (2001) Nabil Ayouch et ses jeux interdits, interview with Nabil Ayouch, <www.lesinrocks.com>.

Mektoub (1997) Written and directed by Nabil Ayouch.

A Minute of Sun Less/Une Minute de soleil en moins (2003) Directed by Nabil Ayouch, written by Malika Al Houback, Nabil Ayouch and Zoubeir Benbouchta.

M'jid, N. (2001) Entretien avec le docteur Najat M'jid, Présidente de l'assocation Bayti, French press booklet.

The Paradise of the Fallen Angels/Fallen Angels Paradise/Gannat Al Shayateen (1999) Directed by Oussama Fawzi, written by Mustapha Zekri, based on Jorge Amado's novel *Dona Flor e seus dois maridos*. Distributed in the US by ArtMattan Productions.

Pixote/Pixote: A Lei do Mais Fraco (1981) Written and directed by Hector Babenco.

Salaam Bombay! (1988) Directed by Mira Nair, written by Sooni Taraporevala.

Samie, A. (2001) Le cinéma marocain s'émancipe, *Maroc hebdo international* 459, 6–12 April, <http://www.maroc-hebdo.press.ma/MHinternet/Archives_459/html_459/cinema.html>.

Saugeon, N. (2001a) *Ali Zaoua, prince de la rue*, Toulouse, Editions Milan.

Saugeon, N. (2001b) L'aventure du tournage vue par . . ., on the French DVD of *Ali Zaoua*.

Saugeon, N. (2001c) Personnages, on the French DVD of *Ali Zaoua*.

Three Kings (1999) Directed by David O. Russell, written by David O. Russell and John Ridley.

Index

For Product Safety Concerns and Information please contact our EU
representative GPSR@taylorandfrancis.com Taylor & Francis Verlag GmbH,
Kaufingerstraße 24, 80331 München, Germany

Batch number: 08153778

Printed by Printforce, the Netherlands